ON WAR
Books One and Two

Carl von Clausewitz

INTRODUCTION FROM THE AUTHOR

That the conception of the scientific does not consist alone, or chiefly, in system, and its finished theoretical constructions, requires nowadays no exposition. System in this treatise is not to be found on the surface, and instead of a finished building of theory, there are only materials.

The scientific form lies here in the endeavour to explore the nature of military phenomena to show their affinity with the nature of the things of which they are composed. Nowhere has the philosophical argument been evaded, but where it runs out into too thin a thread the Author has preferred to cut it short, and fall back upon the corresponding results of experience; for in the same way as many plants only bear fruit when they do not shoot too high, so in the practical arts the theoretical leaves and flowers must not be made to sprout too far, but kept near to experience, which is their proper soil.

Unquestionably it would be a mistake to try to discover from the chemical ingredients of a grain of corn the form of the ear of corn which it bears, as we have only to go to the field to see the ears ripe. Investigation and observation, philosophy and experience, must neither despise nor exclude one another; they mutually afford each other the rights of citizenship. Consequently, the propositions of this book, with their arch of inherent necessity, are supported either by experience or by the conception of War itself as external points, so that they are not without abutments.(*)

(*) That this is not the case in the works of many military writers especially of those who have aimed at treating of War itself in a scientific manner, is shown in many instances, in which by their reasoning, the pro and contra swallow each other up so effectually that there is no vestige of the tails even which were left in the case of the two lions.

It is, perhaps, not impossible to write a systematic theory of War full of spirit and substance, but ours hitherto, have been very much the reverse. To say nothing of their unscientific spirit, in their striving after coherence and completeness of system, they overflow with commonplaces, truisms, and twaddle of every kind. If we want a striking picture of them we have only to read Lichtenberg's extract from a code of regulations in case of fire.

If a house takes fire, we must seek, above all things, to protect the right side of the house standing on the left, and, on the other hand, the left side of the house on the right; for if we, for example, should protect the left side of the house on the left, then the right side of the house lies to the right of the left, and consequently as the fire lies to the right of this side, and of the right side (for we have assumed that the house is situated to the left of the fire), therefore the right side is situated nearer to the fire than the left, and the right side of the house might catch fire if it was not protected before it came to the left, which is protected. Consequently, something might be burnt that is not protected, and that sooner than something else would be burnt, even if it was not protected; consequently we must let alone the latter and protect the former. In order to impress the thing on one's mind, we have only to note if the house is situated to the right of the fire, then it is the left side, and if the house is to the left it is the right side.

In order not to frighten the intelligent reader by such commonplaces, and to make the little good that there is distasteful by pouring water upon it, the Author has preferred to give in small ingots of fine metal his impressions and convictions, the result of many years' reflection on War, of his intercourse with men of ability, and of much personal experience. Thus the seemingly weakly bound-together chapters of this book have arisen, but it is hoped they will not be found wanting in logical connection. Perhaps soon a greater head may appear, and instead of these single grains, give the whole in a casting of pure metal without dross.

BOOK I. ON THE NATURE OF WAR

CHAPTER I. What is War?

1. INTRODUCTION.

We propose to consider first the single elements of our subject, then each branch or part, and, last of all, the whole, in all its relations—therefore to advance from the simple to the complex. But it is necessary for us to commence with a glance at the nature of the whole, because it is particularly necessary that in the consideration of any of the parts their relation to the whole should be kept constantly in view.

2. DEFINITION.

We shall not enter into any of the abstruse definitions of War used by publicists. We shall keep to the element of the thing itself, to a duel. War is nothing but a duel on an extensive scale. If we would conceive as a unit the countless number of duels which make up a War, we shall do so best by supposing to ourselves two wrestlers. Each strives by physical force to compel the other to submit to his will: each endeavours to throw his adversary, and thus render him incapable of further resistance.

War therefore is an act of violence intended to compel our opponent to fulfil our will.

Violence arms itself with the inventions of Art and Science in order to contend against violence. Self-imposed restrictions, almost imperceptible and hardly worth mentioning, termed usages of International Law, accompany it without essentially impairing its power. Violence, that is to say, physical force (for there is no moral force without the conception of States and Law), is therefore the means; the compulsory submission of the enemy to our will is the ultimate object. In order to attain this object fully, the enemy must be disarmed, and disarmament becomes therefore the immediate object of hostilities in theory. It takes the place of the final object, and puts it aside as something we can eliminate from our calculations.

3. UTMOST USE OF FORCE.

Now, philanthropists may easily imagine there is a skilful method of disarming and overcoming an enemy without great bloodshed, and that this is the proper tendency of the Art of War. However plausible this may appear, still it is an error which must be extirpated; for in such dangerous things as War, the errors which proceed from a spirit of benevolence are the worst. As the use of physical power to the utmost extent by no means excludes the co-operation of the intelligence, it follows that he who uses force unsparingly, without reference to the bloodshed involved, must obtain a superiority if his adversary uses less vigour in its application. The former then dictates the law to the latter, and both proceed to extremities to which the only limitations are those imposed by the amount of counter-acting force on each side.

This is the way in which the matter must be viewed and it is to no purpose, it is even against one's own interest, to turn away from the consideration of the real nature of the affair because the horror of its elements excites repugnance.

If the Wars of civilised people are less cruel and destructive than those of savages, the difference arises from the social condition both of States in themselves and in their relations to each other. Out of this social condition and its relations War arises, and by it War is subjected to conditions, is controlled and modified. But these things do not belong to War itself; they are only given conditions; and to introduce into the philosophy of War itself a principle of moderation would be an absurdity.

Two motives lead men to War: instinctive hostility and hostile intention. In our definition of War, we have chosen as its characteristic the latter of these elements, because it is the most general. It is impossible to conceive the passion of hatred of the wildest description, bordering on mere instinct, without combining with it the idea of a hostile intention. On the other hand, hostile intentions may often exist without being accompanied by any, or at all events by any extreme, hostility of feeling. Amongst savages views emanating from the feelings, amongst civilised nations those emanating from the understanding, have the predominance; but this difference arises from attendant circumstances, existing institutions, &c., and, therefore, is not to be found necessarily in all cases, although it prevails in the majority. In short, even the most civilised nations may burn with passionate hatred of each other.

We may see from this what a fallacy it would be to refer the War of a civilised nation entirely to an intelligent act on the part of the Government, and to imagine it as continually freeing itself more and more from all feeling of passion in such a way that at last the physical masses of combatants would no longer be required; in reality, their mere relations would suffice—a kind of algebraic action.

Theory was beginning to drift in this direction until the facts of the last War(*) taught it better. If War is an act of force, it belongs necessarily also to the feelings. If it does not originate in the feelings, it reacts, more or less, upon them, and the extent of this reaction depends not on the degree of civilisation, but upon the importance and duration of the interests involved.

(*) Clausewitz alludes here to the "Wars of Liberation," 1813, 14, 15.

Therefore, if we find civilised nations do not put their prisoners to death, do not devastate towns and countries, this is because their intelligence exercises greater influence on their mode of carrying on War, and has taught them more effectual means of applying force than these rude acts of mere instinct. The invention of gunpowder, the constant progress of improvements in the construction of firearms, are sufficient proofs that the tendency to destroy the adversary which lies at the bottom of the conception of War is in no way changed or modified through the progress of civilisation.

We therefore repeat our proposition, that War is an act of violence pushed to its utmost bounds; as one side dictates the law to the other, there arises a sort of reciprocal action, which logically must lead to an extreme. This is the first reciprocal action, and the first extreme with which we meet (first reciprocal action).

4. THE AIM IS TO DISARM THE ENEMY.

We have already said that the aim of all action in War is to disarm the enemy, and we shall now show that this, theoretically at least, is indispensable.

If our opponent is to be made to comply with our will, we must place him in a situation which is more oppressive to him than the sacrifice which we demand; but the disadvantages of this position must naturally not be of a transitory nature, at least in appearance, otherwise the enemy, instead of yielding, will hold out, in the prospect of a change for the better. Every change in this position which is produced by a continuation of the War should therefore be a change for the worse. The worst condition in which a belligerent can be placed is that of being completely disarmed. If, therefore, the enemy is to be reduced to submission by an act of War, he must either be positively disarmed or placed in such a position that he is threatened with it. From this it follows that the disarming or overthrow of the enemy, whichever we call it, must always be the aim of Warfare. Now War is always the shock of two hostile bodies in collision, not the action of a living power upon an inanimate mass, because an absolute state of endurance would not be making War; therefore, what we have just said as to the aim of action in War applies to both parties. Here, then, is another case of reciprocal action. As long as the enemy is not defeated, he may defeat me; then I shall be no longer my own master; he will dictate the law to me as I did to him. This is the second reciprocal action, and leads to a second extreme (second reciprocal action).

5. UTMOST EXERTION OF POWERS.

If we desire to defeat the enemy, we must proportion our efforts to his powers of resistance. This is expressed by the product of two factors which cannot be separated, namely, the sum of available means and the strength of the Will. The sum of the available means may be estimated in a measure, as it depends (although not entirely) upon numbers; but the strength of volition is more difficult to determine, and can only be estimated to a certain extent by the strength of the motives. Granted we have obtained in this way an approximation to the strength of the power to be contended with, we can then take of our own means, and either increase them so as to obtain a preponderance, or, in case we have not the resources to effect this, then do our best by increasing our means as far as possible. But the adversary does the same; therefore, there is a new mutual enhancement, which, in pure conception, must create a fresh effort towards an extreme. This is the third case of reciprocal action, and a third extreme with which we meet (third reciprocal action).

6. MODIFICATION IN THE REALITY.

Thus reasoning in the abstract, the mind cannot stop short of an extreme, because it has to deal with an extreme, with a conflict of forces left to themselves, and obeying no other but their own inner laws. If we should seek to deduce from the pure conception of War an absolute point for the aim which we shall propose and for the means which we shall apply, this constant reciprocal action would involve us in extremes, which would be nothing but a play of ideas produced by an almost invisible train of logical subtleties. If, adhering closely to the absolute, we try to avoid all difficulties by a stroke of the pen, and insist with logical strictness that in every case the extreme must be the object, and the utmost effort must be exerted in that direction, such a stroke of the pen would be a mere paper law, not by any means adapted to the real world.

Even supposing this extreme tension of forces was an absolute which could easily be ascertained, still we must admit that the human mind would hardly submit itself to this kind of logical chimera. There would be in many cases an unnecessary waste of power, which would be in opposition to other principles of statecraft; an effort of Will would be required disproportioned to the proposed object, which therefore it would be impossible to realise, for the human will does not derive its impulse from logical subtleties.

But everything takes a different shape when we pass from abstractions to reality. In the former, everything must be subject to optimism, and we must imagine the one side as well as the other striving after perfection and even attaining it. Will this ever take place in reality? It will if,

(1) War becomes a completely isolated act, which arises suddenly, and is in no way connected with the previous history of the combatant States.

(2) If it is limited to a single solution, or to several simultaneous solutions.

(3) If it contains within itself the solution perfect and complete, free from any reaction upon it, through a calculation beforehand of the political situation which will follow from it.

7. WAR IS NEVER AN ISOLATED ACT.

With regard to the first point, neither of the two opponents is an abstract person to the other, not even as regards that factor in the sum of resistance which does not depend on objective things, viz., the Will. This Will is not an entirely unknown quantity; it indicates what it will be to-morrow by what it is to-day. War does not spring up quite suddenly, it does not spread to the full in a moment; each of the two opponents can, therefore, form an opinion of the other, in a great measure, from what he is and what he does, instead of judging of him according to what he, strictly speaking, should be or should do. But, now, man with his incomplete organisation is always below the line of absolute perfection, and thus these deficiencies, having an influence on both sides, become a modifying principle.

8. WAR DOES NOT CONSIST OF A SINGLE INSTANTANEOUS BLOW.

The second point gives rise to the following considerations:—

If War ended in a single solution, or a number of simultaneous ones, then naturally all the preparations for the same would have a tendency to the extreme, for an omission could not in any way be repaired; the utmost, then, that the world of reality could furnish as a guide for us would be the preparations of the enemy, as far as they are known to us; all the rest would fall into the domain of the abstract. But if the result is made up from several successive acts, then naturally that which precedes with all its phases may be taken as a measure for that which will follow, and in this manner the world of reality again takes the place of the abstract, and thus modifies the effort towards the extreme.

Yet every War would necessarily resolve itself into a single solution, or a sum of simultaneous results, if all the means required for the struggle were raised at once, or could be at once raised; for as one adverse result necessarily diminishes the means, then if all the means have been applied in the first, a second cannot properly be supposed. All hostile acts which might follow would belong essentially to the first, and form, in reality only its duration.

But we have already seen that even in the preparation for War the real world steps into the place of mere abstract conception—a material standard into the place of the hypotheses of an extreme: that therefore in that way both parties, by the influence of the mutual reaction, remain below the line of extreme effort, and therefore all forces are not at once brought forward.

It lies also in the nature of these forces and their application that they cannot all be brought into activity at the same time. These forces are the armies actually on foot, the country, with its superficial extent and its population, and the allies.

In point of fact, the country, with its superficial area and the population, besides being the source of all military force, constitutes in itself an integral part of the efficient quantities in War, providing either the theatre of war or exercising a considerable influence on the same.

Now, it is possible to bring all the movable military forces of a country into operation at once, but not all fortresses, rivers, mountains, people, &c.—in short, not the whole country, unless it is so small that it may be completely embraced by the first act of the War. Further, the co-operation of allies does not depend on the Will of the belligerents; and from the nature of the political relations of states to each other, this co-operation is frequently not afforded until after the War has commenced, or it may be increased to restore the balance of power.

That this part of the means of resistance, which cannot at once be brought into activity, in many cases, is a much greater part of the whole than might at first be supposed, and that it often restores the balance of power, seriously affected by the great force of the first decision, will be more fully shown hereafter. Here it is sufficient to show that a complete concentration of all available means in a moment of time is contradictory to the nature of War.

Now this, in itself, furnishes no ground for relaxing our efforts to accumulate strength to gain the first result, because an unfavourable issue is always a disadvantage to which no one would purposely expose himself, and also because the first decision, although not the only one, still will have the more influence on subsequent events, the greater it is in itself.

But the possibility of gaining a later result causes men to take refuge in that expectation, owing to the repugnance in the human mind to making excessive efforts; and therefore forces are not concentrated and measures are not taken for the first decision with that energy which would otherwise be used. Whatever one belligerent omits from weakness, becomes to the other a real objective ground for limiting his own efforts, and thus again, through this reciprocal action, extreme tendencies are brought down to efforts on a limited scale.

9. THE RESULT IN WAR IS NEVER ABSOLUTE.

Lastly, even the final decision of a whole War is not always to be regarded as absolute. The conquered State often sees in it only a passing evil, which may be repaired in after times by means of political combinations. How much this must modify the degree of tension, and the vigour of the efforts made, is evident in itself.

10. THE PROBABILITIES OF REAL LIFE TAKE THE PLACE OF THE CONCEPTIONS OF THE EXTREME AND THE ABSOLUTE.

In this manner, the whole act of War is removed from the rigorous law of forces exerted to the utmost. If the extreme is no longer to be apprehended, and no longer to be sought for, it is left to the judgment to determine the limits for the efforts to be made in place of it, and this can only be done on the data furnished by the facts of the real world by the LAWS OF PROBABILITY. Once the belligerents are no longer mere conceptions, but individual States and Governments, once the War is no longer an ideal, but a definite substantial procedure, then the reality will furnish the data to compute the unknown quantities which are required to be found.

From the character, the measures, the situation of the adversary, and the relations with which he is surrounded, each side will draw conclusions by the law of probability as to the designs of the other, and act accordingly.

11. THE POLITICAL OBJECT NOW REAPPEARS.

Here the question which we had laid aside forces itself again into consideration (see No. 2), viz., the political object of the War. The law of the extreme, the view to disarm the adversary, to overthrow him, has hitherto to a certain extent usurped the place of this end or object. Just as this law loses its force, the political must again come forward. If the whole consideration is a calculation of probability based on definite persons and relations, then the political object, being the original motive, must be an essential factor in the product. The smaller the sacrifice we demand from ours, the smaller, it may be expected, will be the means of resistance which he will employ; but the smaller his preparation, the smaller will ours require to be. Further, the smaller our political object, the less value shall we set upon it, and the more easily shall we be induced to give it up altogether.

Thus, therefore, the political object, as the original motive of the War, will be the standard for determining both the aim of the military force and also the amount of effort to be made. This it cannot be in itself, but it is so in relation to both the belligerent States, because we are concerned with realities, not with mere abstractions. One and the same political object may produce totally different effects upon different people, or even upon the same people at different times; we can, therefore, only admit the political object as the measure, by considering it in its effects upon those masses which it is to move, and consequently the nature of those masses also comes into consideration. It is easy to see that thus the result may be very different according as these masses are animated with a spirit which will infuse vigour into the action or otherwise. It is quite possible for such a state of feeling to exist between two States that a very trifling political motive for War may produce an effect quite disproportionate—in fact, a perfect explosion.

This applies to the efforts which the political object will call forth in the two States, and to the aim which the military action shall prescribe for itself. At times it may itself be that aim, as, for example, the conquest of a province. At other times the political object itself is not suitable for the aim of military action; then such a one must be chosen as will be an equivalent for it, and stand in its place as regards the conclusion of peace. But also, in this, due attention to the peculiar character of the States concerned is always supposed. There are circumstances in which the equivalent must be much greater than the political object, in order to secure the latter. The political object will be so much the more the standard of aim and effort, and have more influence in itself, the more the masses are indifferent, the less that any mutual feeling of hostility prevails in the two States from other causes, and therefore there are cases where the political object almost alone will be decisive.

If the aim of the military action is an equivalent for the political object, that action will in general diminish as the political object diminishes, and in a greater degree the more the political object dominates. Thus it is explained how, without any contradiction in itself, there may be Wars of all degrees of importance and energy, from a War of extermination down to the mere use of an army of observation. This, however, leads to a question of another kind which we have hereafter to develop and answer.

12. A SUSPENSION IN THE ACTION OF WAR UNEXPLAINED BY ANYTHING SAID AS YET.

However insignificant the political claims mutually advanced, however weak the means put forth, however small the aim to which military action is directed, can this action be suspended even for a moment? This is a question which penetrates deeply into the nature of the subject.

Every transaction requires for its accomplishment a certain time which we call its duration. This may be longer or shorter, according as the person acting throws more or less despatch into his movements.

About this more or less we shall not trouble ourselves here. Each person acts in his own fashion; but the slow person does not protract the thing because he wishes to spend more time about it, but because by his nature he requires more time, and if he made more haste would not do the thing so well. This time, therefore, depends on subjective causes, and belongs to the length, so called, of the action.

If we allow now to every action in War this, its length, then we must assume, at first sight at least, that any expenditure of time beyond this length, that is, every suspension of hostile action, appears an absurdity; with respect to this it must not be forgotten that we now speak not of the progress of one or other of the two opponents, but of the general progress of the whole action of the War.

13. THERE IS ONLY ONE CAUSE WHICH CAN SUSPEND THE ACTION, AND THIS SEEMS TO BE ONLY POSSIBLE ON ONE SIDE IN ANY CASE.

If two parties have armed themselves for strife, then a feeling of animosity must have moved them to it; as long now as they continue armed, that is, do not come to terms of peace, this feeling must exist; and it can only be brought to a standstill by either side by one single motive alone, which is, THAT HE WAITS FOR A MORE FAVOURABLE MOMENT FOR ACTION. Now, at first sight, it appears that this motive can never exist except on one side, because it, eo ipso, must be prejudicial to the other. If the one has an interest in acting, then the other must have an interest in waiting.

A complete equilibrium of forces can never produce a suspension of action, for during this suspension he who has the positive object (that is, the assailant) must continue progressing; for if we should imagine an equilibrium in this way, that he who has the positive object, therefore the strongest motive, can at the same time only command the lesser means, so that the equation is made up by the product of the motive and the power, then we must say, if no alteration in this condition of equilibrium is to be expected, the two parties must make peace; but if an alteration is to be expected, then it can only be favourable to one side, and therefore the other has a manifest interest to act without delay. We see that the conception of an equilibrium cannot explain a suspension of arms, but that it ends in the question of the EXPECTATION OF A MORE FAVOURABLE MOMENT.

Let us suppose, therefore, that one of two States has a positive object, as, for instance, the conquest of one of the enemy's provinces—which is to be utilised in the settlement of peace. After this conquest, his political object is accomplished, the necessity for action ceases, and for him a pause ensues. If the adversary is also contented with this solution, he will make peace; if not, he must act. Now, if we suppose that in four weeks he will be in a better condition to act, then he has sufficient grounds for putting off the time of action.

But from that moment the logical course for the enemy appears to be to act that he may not give the conquered party THE DESIRED time. Of course, in this mode of reasoning a complete insight into the state of circumstances on both sides is supposed.

14. THUS A CONTINUANCE OF ACTION WILL ENSUE WHICH WILL ADVANCE TOWARDS A CLIMAX.

If this unbroken continuity of hostile operations really existed, the effect would be that everything would again be driven towards the extreme; for, irrespective of the effect of such incessant activity in inflaming the feelings, and infusing into the whole a greater degree of passion, a greater elementary force, there would also follow from this continuance of action a stricter continuity, a closer connection between cause and effect, and thus every single action would become of more importance, and consequently more replete with danger.

But we know that the course of action in War has seldom or never this unbroken continuity, and that there have been many Wars in which action occupied by far the smallest portion of time employed, the whole of the rest being consumed in inaction. It is impossible that this should be always an anomaly; suspension of action in War must therefore be possible, that is no contradiction in itself. We now proceed to show how this is.

15. HERE, THEREFORE, THE PRINCIPLE OF POLARITY IS BROUGHT INTO REQUISITION.

As we have supposed the interests of one Commander to be always antagonistic to those of the other, we have assumed a true polarity. We reserve a fuller explanation of this for another chapter, merely making the following observation on it at present.

The principle of polarity is only valid when it can be conceived in one and the same thing, where the positive and its opposite the negative completely destroy each other. In a battle both sides strive to conquer; that is true polarity, for the victory of the one side destroys that of the other. But when we speak of two different things which have a common relation external to themselves, then it is not the things but their relations which have the polarity.

16. ATTACK AND DEFENCE ARE THINGS DIFFERING IN KIND AND OF UNEQUAL FORCE. POLARITY IS, THEREFORE, NOT APPLICABLE TO THEM.

If there was only one form of War, to wit, the attack of the enemy, therefore no defence; or, in other words, if the attack was distinguished from the defence merely by the positive motive, which the one has and the other has not, but the methods of each were precisely one and the same: then in this sort of fight every advantage gained on the one side would be a corresponding disadvantage on the other, and true polarity would exist.

But action in War is divided into two forms, attack and defence, which, as we shall hereafter explain more particularly, are very different and of unequal strength. Polarity therefore lies in that to which both bear a relation, in the decision, but not in the attack or defence itself.

If the one Commander wishes the solution put off, the other must wish to hasten it, but only by the same form of action. If it is A's interest not to attack his enemy at present, but four weeks hence, then it is B's interest to be attacked, not four weeks hence, but at the present moment. This is the direct antagonism of interests, but it by no means follows that it would be for B's interest to attack A at once. That is plainly something totally different.

17. THE EFFECT OF POLARITY IS OFTEN DESTROYED BY THE SUPERIORITY OF THE DEFENCE OVER THE ATTACK,

AND THUS THE SUSPENSION OF ACTION IN WAR IS EXPLAINED.

If the form of defence is stronger than that of offence, as we shall hereafter show, the question arises, Is the advantage of a deferred decision as great on the one side as the advantage of the defensive form on the other? If it is not, then it cannot by its counter-weight over-balance the latter, and thus influence the progress of the action of the War. We see, therefore, that the impulsive force existing in the polarity of interests may be lost in the difference between the strength of the offensive and the defensive, and thereby become ineffectual.

If, therefore, that side for which the present is favourable, is too weak to be able to dispense with the advantage of the defensive, he must put up with the unfavourable prospects which the future holds out; for it may still be better to fight a defensive battle in the unpromising future than to assume the offensive or make peace at present. Now, being convinced that the superiority of the defensive(*) (rightly understood) is very great, and much greater than may appear at first sight, we conceive that the greater number of those periods of inaction which occur in war are thus explained without involving any contradiction. The weaker the motives to action are, the more will those motives be absorbed and neutralised by this difference between attack and defence, the more frequently, therefore, will action in warfare be stopped, as indeed experience teaches.

(*) It must be remembered that all this antedates by some years the introduction of long-range weapons.

18 A SECOND GROUND CONSISTS IN THE IMPERFECT KNOWLEDGE OF CIRCUMSTANCES.

But there is still another cause which may stop action in War, viz., an incomplete view of the situation. Each Commander can only fully know his own position; that of his opponent can only be known to him by reports, which are uncertain; he may, therefore, form a wrong judgment with respect to it upon data of this description, and, in consequence of that error, he may suppose that the power of taking the initiative rests with his adversary when it lies really with himself. This want of perfect insight might certainly just as often occasion an untimely action as untimely inaction, and hence it would in itself no more contribute to delay than to accelerate action in War. Still, it must always be regarded as one of the natural causes which may bring action in War to a standstill without involving a contradiction. But if we reflect how much more we are inclined and induced to estimate the power of our opponents too high than too low, because it lies in human nature to do so, we shall admit that our imperfect insight into facts in general must contribute very much to delay action in War, and to modify the application of the principles pending our conduct.

The possibility of a standstill brings into the action of War a new modification, inasmuch as it dilutes that action with the element of time, checks the influence or sense of danger in its course, and increases the means of reinstating a lost balance of force. The greater the tension of feelings from which the War springs, the greater therefore the energy with which it is carried on, so much the shorter will be the periods of inaction; on the other hand, the weaker the principle of warlike activity, the longer will be these periods: for powerful motives increase the force of the will, and this, as we know, is always a factor in the product of force.

19. FREQUENT PERIODS OF INACTION IN WAR REMOVE IT FURTHER FROM THE ABSOLUTE, AND MAKE IT STILL MORE A CALCULATION OF PROBABILITIES.

But the slower the action proceeds in War, the more frequent and longer the periods of inaction, so much the more easily can an error be repaired; therefore, so much the bolder a General will be in his calculations, so much the more readily will he keep them below the line of the absolute, and build everything upon probabilities and conjecture. Thus, according as the course of the

War is more or less slow, more or less time will be allowed for that which the nature of a concrete case particularly requires, calculation of probability based on given circumstances.

20. THEREFORE, THE ELEMENT OF CHANCE ONLY IS WANTING TO MAKE OF WAR A GAME, AND IN THAT ELEMENT IT IS LEAST OF ALL DEFICIENT.

We see from the foregoing how much the objective nature of War makes it a calculation of probabilities; now there is only one single element still wanting to make it a game, and that element it certainly is not without: it is chance. There is no human affair which stands so constantly and so generally in close connection with chance as War. But together with chance, the accidental, and along with it good luck, occupy a great place in War.

21. WAR IS A GAME BOTH OBJECTIVELY AND SUBJECTIVELY.

If we now take a look at the subjective nature of War, that is to say, at those conditions under which it is carried on, it will appear to us still more like a game. Primarily the element in which the operations of War are carried on is danger; but which of all the moral qualities is the first in danger? Courage. Now certainly courage is quite compatible with prudent calculation, but still they are things of quite a different kind, essentially different qualities of the mind; on the other hand, daring reliance on good fortune, boldness, rashness, are only expressions of courage, and all these propensities of the mind look for the fortuitous (or accidental), because it is their element.

We see, therefore, how, from the commencement, the absolute, the mathematical as it is called, nowhere finds any sure basis in the calculations in the Art of War; and that from the outset there is a play of possibilities, probabilities, good and bad luck, which spreads about with all the coarse and fine threads of its web, and makes War of all branches of human activity the most like a gambling game.

22. HOW THIS ACCORDS BEST WITH THE HUMAN MIND IN GENERAL.

Although our intellect always feels itself urged towards clearness and certainty, still our mind often feels itself attracted by uncertainty. Instead of threading its way with the understanding along the narrow path of philosophical investigations and logical conclusions, in order, almost unconscious of itself, to arrive in spaces where it feels itself a stranger, and where it seems to part from all well-known objects, it prefers to remain with the imagination in the realms of chance and luck. Instead of living yonder on poor necessity, it revels here in the wealth of possibilities; animated thereby, courage then takes wings to itself, and daring and danger make the element into which it launches itself as a fearless swimmer plunges into the stream.

Shall theory leave it here, and move on, self-satisfied with absolute conclusions and rules? Then it is of no practical use. Theory must also take into account the human element; it must accord a place to courage, to boldness, even to rashness. The Art of War has to deal with living and with moral forces, the consequence of which is that it can never attain the absolute and positive. There is therefore everywhere a margin for the accidental, and just as much in the greatest things as in the smallest. As there is room for this accidental on the one hand, so on the other there must be courage and self-reliance in proportion to the room available. If these qualities are forthcoming in a high degree, the margin left may likewise be great. Courage and self-reliance are, therefore, principles quite essential to War; consequently, theory must only set up such rules as allow ample scope for all degrees and varieties of these necessary and noblest of military virtues. In daring there may still be wisdom, and prudence as well, only they are estimated by a different standard of value.

23. WAR IS ALWAYS A SERIOUS MEANS FOR A SERIOUS OBJECT. ITS MORE PARTICULAR DEFINITION.

Such is War; such the Commander who conducts it; such the theory which rules it. But War is no pastime; no mere passion for venturing and winning; no work of a free enthusiasm: it is a serious means for a serious object. All that appearance which it wears from the varying hues of fortune, all that it assimilates into itself of the oscillations of passion, of courage, of imagination, of enthusiasm, are only particular properties of this means.

The War of a community—of whole Nations, and particularly of civilised Nations—always starts from a political condition, and is called forth by a political motive. It is, therefore, a political act. Now if it was a perfect, unrestrained, and absolute expression of force, as we had to deduct it from its mere conception, then the moment it is called forth by policy it would step into the place of policy, and as something quite independent of it would set it aside, and only follow its own laws, just as a mine at the moment of explosion cannot be guided into any other direction than that which has been given to it by preparatory arrangements. This is how the thing has really been viewed hitherto, whenever a want of harmony between policy and the conduct of a War has led to theoretical distinctions of the kind. But it is not so, and the idea is radically false. War in the real world, as we have already seen, is not an extreme thing which expends itself at one single discharge; it is the operation of powers which do not develop themselves completely in the same manner and in the same measure, but which at one time expand sufficiently to overcome the resistance opposed by inertia or friction, while at another they are too weak to produce an effect; it is therefore, in a certain measure, a pulsation of violent force more or less vehement, consequently making its discharges and exhausting its powers more or less quickly—in other words, conducting more or less quickly to the aim, but always lasting long enough to admit of influence being exerted on it in its course, so as to give it this or that direction, in short, to be subject to the will of a guiding intelligence., if we reflect that War has its root in a political object, then naturally this original motive which called it into existence should also continue the first and highest consideration in its conduct. Still, the political object is no despotic lawgiver on that account; it must accommodate itself to the nature of the means, and though changes in these means may involve modification in the political objective, the latter always retains a prior right to consideration. Policy, therefore, is interwoven with the whole action of War, and must exercise a continuous influence upon it, as far as the nature of the forces liberated by it will permit.

24. WAR IS A MERE CONTINUATION OF POLICY BY OTHER MEANS.

We see, therefore, that War is not merely a political act, but also a real political instrument, a continuation of political commerce, a carrying out of the same by other means. All beyond this which is strictly peculiar to War relates merely to the peculiar nature of the means which it uses. That the tendencies and views of policy shall not be incompatible with these means, the Art of War in general and the Commander in each particular case may demand, and this claim is truly not a trifling one. But however powerfully this may react on political views in particular cases, still it must always be regarded as only a modification of them; for the political view is the object, War is the means, and the means must always include the object in our conception.

25. DIVERSITY IN THE NATURE OF WARS.

The greater and the more powerful the motives of a War, the more it affects the whole existence of a people. The more violent the excitement which precedes the War, by so much the nearer will the War approach to its abstract form, so much the more will it be directed to the destruction of the enemy, so much the nearer will the military and political ends coincide, so much the more purely military and less political the War appears to be; but the weaker the motives and the tensions, so much the less will the natural direction of the military element—that is, force—be coincident with the direction which the political element indicates; so much the more must, therefore, the War become diverted from its natural direction, the political object diverge from the aim of an ideal War, and the War appear to become political.

But, that the reader may not form any false conceptions, we must here observe that by this natural tendency of War we only mean the philosophical, the strictly logical, and by no means the tendency of forces actually engaged in conflict, by which would be supposed to be included all the emotions and passions of the combatants. No doubt in some cases these also might be excited to such a degree as to be with difficulty restrained and confined to the political road; but in most cases such a contradiction will not arise, because by the existence of such strenuous exertions a great plan in harmony therewith would be implied. If the plan is directed only upon a small object, then the impulses of feeling amongst the masses will be also so weak that these masses will require to be stimulated rather than repressed.

26. THEY MAY ALL BE REGARDED AS POLITICAL ACTS.

Returning now to the main subject, although it is true that in one kind of War the political element seems almost to disappear, whilst in another kind it occupies a very prominent place, we may still affirm that the one is as political as the other; for if we regard the State policy as the intelligence of the personified State, then amongst all the constellations in the political sky whose movements it has to compute, those must be included which arise when the nature of its relations imposes the necessity of a great War. It is only if we understand by policy not a true appreciation of affairs in general, but the conventional conception of a cautious, subtle, also dishonest craftiness, averse from violence, that the latter kind of War may belong more to policy than the first.

27. INFLUENCE OF THIS VIEW ON THE RIGHT UNDERSTANDING OF MILITARY HISTORY, AND ON THE FOUNDATIONS OF THEORY.

We see, therefore, in the first place, that under all circumstances War is to be regarded not as an independent thing, but as a political instrument; and it is only by taking this point of view that we can avoid finding ourselves in opposition to all military history. This is the only means of unlocking the great book and making it intelligible. Secondly, this view shows us how Wars must differ in character according to the nature of the motives and circumstances from which they proceed.

Now, the first, the grandest, and most decisive act of judgment which the Statesman and General exercises is rightly to understand in this respect the War in which he engages, not to take it for something, or to wish to make of it something, which by the nature of its relations it is impossible for it to be. This is, therefore, the first, the most comprehensive, of all strategical questions. We shall enter into this more fully in treating of the plan of a War.

For the present we content ourselves with having brought the subject up to this point, and having thereby fixed the chief point of view from which War and its theory are to be studied.

28. RESULT FOR THEORY.

War is, therefore, not only chameleon-like in character, because it changes its colour in some degree in each particular case, but it is also, as a whole, in relation to the predominant tendencies which are in it, a wonderful trinity, composed of the original violence of its elements, hatred and animosity, which may be looked upon as blind instinct; of the play of probabilities and chance, which make it a free activity of the soul; and of the subordinate nature of a political instrument, by which it belongs purely to the reason.

The first of these three phases concerns more the people the second, more the General and his Army; the third, more the Government. The passions which break forth in War must already have a latent existence in the peoples. The range which the display of courage and talents shall get in the realm of probabilities and of chance depends on the particular characteristics of the General and his Army, but the political objects belong to the Government alone.

These three tendencies, which appear like so many different law-givers, are deeply rooted in the nature of the subject, and at the same time variable in degree. A theory which would leave any one of them out of account, or set up any arbitrary relation between them, would immediately become involved in such a contradiction with the reality, that it might be regarded as destroyed at once by that alone.

The problem is, therefore, that theory shall keep itself poised in a manner between these three tendencies, as between three points of attraction.

The way in which alone this difficult problem can be solved we shall examine in the book on the "Theory of War." In every case the conception of War, as here defined, will be the first ray of light which shows us the true foundation of theory, and which first separates the great masses and allows us to distinguish them from one another.

CHAPTER II. Ends and Means in War

Having in the foregoing chapter ascertained the complicated and variable nature of War, we shall now occupy ourselves in examining into the influence which this nature has upon the end and means in War.

If we ask, first of all, for the object upon which the whole effort of War is to be directed, in order that it may suffice for the attainment of the political object, we shall find that it is just as variable as are the political object and the particular circumstances of the War.

If, in the next place, we keep once more to the pure conception of War, then we must say that the political object properly lies out of its province, for if War is an act of violence to compel the enemy to fulfil our will, then in every case all depends on our overthrowing the enemy, that is, disarming him, and on that alone. This object, developed from abstract conceptions, but which is also the one aimed at in a great many cases in reality, we shall, in the first place, examine in this reality.

In connection with the plan of a campaign we shall hereafter examine more closely into the meaning of disarming a nation, but here we must at once draw a distinction between three things, which, as three general objects, comprise everything else within them. They are the military power, the country, and the will of the enemy.

The military power must be destroyed, that is, reduced to such a state as not to be able to prosecute the War. This is the sense in which we wish to be understood hereafter, whenever we use the expression "destruction of the enemy's military power."

The country must be conquered, for out of the country a new military force may be formed.

But even when both these things are done, still the War, that is, the hostile feeling and action of hostile agencies, cannot be considered as at an end as long as the will of the enemy is not subdued also; that is, its Government and its Allies must be forced into signing a peace, or the people into submission; for whilst we are in full occupation of the country, the War may break out afresh, either in the interior or through assistance given by Allies. No doubt, this may also take place after a peace, but that shows nothing more than that every War does not carry in itself the elements for a complete decision and final settlement.

But even if this is the case, still with the conclusion of peace a number of sparks are always extinguished which would have smouldered on quietly, and the excitement of the passions abates, because all those whose minds are disposed to peace, of which in all nations and under all circumstances there is always a great number, turn themselves away completely from the road to resistance. Whatever may take place subsequently, we must always look upon the object as attained, and the business of War as ended, by a peace.

As protection of the country is the primary object for which the military force exists, therefore the natural order is, that first of all this force should be destroyed, then the country subdued; and through the effect of these two results, as well as the position we then hold, the enemy should be forced to make peace. Generally the destruction of the enemy's force is done by degrees, and in just the same measure the conquest of the country follows immediately. The two likewise usually react upon each other, because the loss of provinces occasions a diminution of military force. But this order is by no means necessary, and on that account it also does not always take place. The enemy's Army, before it is sensibly weakened, may retreat to the opposite side of the country, or even quite outside of it. In this case, therefore, the greater part or the whole of the country is conquered.

But this object of War in the abstract, this final means of attaining the political object in which all others are combined, the disarming the enemy, is rarely attained in practice and is not a condition necessary to peace. Therefore it can in no wise be set up in theory as a law. There are innumerable instances of treaties in which peace has been settled before either party could be looked upon as disarmed; indeed, even before the balance of power had undergone any sensible alteration. Nay, further, if we look at the case in the concrete, then we must say that in a whole class of cases, the idea of a complete defeat of the enemy would be a mere imaginative flight, especially when the enemy is considerably superior.

The reason why the object deduced from the conception of War is not adapted in general to real War lies in the difference between the two, which is discussed in the preceding chapter. If it was as pure theory gives it, then a War between two States of very unequal military strength would appear an absurdity; therefore impossible. At most, the inequality between the physical forces might be such that it could be balanced by the moral forces, and that would not go far with our present social condition in Europe. Therefore, if we have seen Wars take place between States of very unequal power, that has been the case because there is a wide difference between War in reality and its original conception.

There are two considerations which as motives may practically take the place of inability to continue the contest. The first is the improbability, the second is the excessive price, of success.

According to what we have seen in the foregoing chapter, War must always set itself free from the strict law of logical necessity, and seek aid from the calculation of probabilities; and as this is so much the more the case, the more the War has a bias that way, from the circumstances out of which it has arisen—the smaller its motives are, and the excitement it has raised—so it is also conceivable how out of this calculation of probabilities even motives to peace may arise. War does not, therefore, always require to be fought out until one party is overthrown; and we may suppose that, when the motives and passions are slight, a weak probability will suffice to move that side to which it is unfavourable to give way. Now, were the other side convinced of this beforehand, it is natural that he would strive for this probability only, instead of first wasting time and effort in the attempt to achieve the total destruction of the enemy's Army.

Still more general in its influence on the resolution to peace is the consideration of the expenditure of force already made, and further required. As War is no act of blind passion, but is dominated by the political object, therefore the value of that object determines the measure of the sacrifices by which it is to be purchased. This will be the case, not only as regards extent, but also as regards duration. As soon, therefore, as the required outlay becomes so great that the political object is no longer equal in value, the object must be given up, and peace will be the result.

We see, therefore, that in Wars where one side cannot completely disarm the other, the motives to peace on both sides will rise or fall on each side according to the probability of future success and the required outlay. If these motives were equally strong on both sides, they would meet in the centre of their political difference. Where they are strong on one side, they might be weak on the other. If their amount is only sufficient, peace will follow, but naturally to the advantage of that side which has the weakest motive for its conclusion. We purposely pass over here the difference which the positive and negative character of the political end must necessarily produce practically; for although that is, as we shall hereafter show, of the highest importance, still we are obliged to keep here to a more general point of view, because the original political views in the course of the War change very much, and at last may become totally different, just because they are determined by results and probable events.

Now comes the question how to influence the probability of success. In the first place, naturally by the same means which we use when the object is the subjugation of the enemy, by the destruction of his military force and the conquest of his provinces; but these two means are not exactly of the same import here as they would be in reference to that object. If we attack the enemy's Army, it is a very different thing whether we intend to follow up the first blow with a succession of others, until the whole force is destroyed, or whether we mean to content ourselves with a victory to shake the enemy's feeling of security, to convince him of our superiority, and to instil into him a feeling of apprehension about the future. If this is our object, we only go so far in the destruction of his forces as is sufficient. In like manner, the conquest, of the enemy's provinces is quite a different measure if the object is not the destruction of the enemy's Army. In the latter case the destruction of the Army is the real effectual action, and the taking of the provinces only a consequence of it; to take them before the Army had been defeated would always be looked upon only as a necessary evil. On the other hand, if our views are not directed upon the complete destruction of the enemy's force, and if we are sure that the enemy does not seek but fears to bring matters to a bloody decision, the taking possession of a weak or defenceless province is an advantage in itself, and if this advantage is of sufficient importance to make the enemy apprehensive about the general result, then it may also be regarded as a shorter road to peace.

But now we come upon a peculiar means of influencing the probability of the result without destroying the enemy's Army, namely, upon the expeditions which have a direct connection with political views. If there are any enterprises which are particularly likely to break up the enemy's alliances or make them inoperative, to gain new alliances for ourselves, to raise political powers in our own favour, &c. &c., then it is easy to conceive how much these may increase the probability of success, and become a shorter way towards our object than the routing of the enemy's forces.

The second question is how to act upon the enemy's expenditure in strength, that is, to raise the price of success.

The enemy's outlay in strength lies in the wear and tear of his forces, consequently in the destruction of them on our part, and in the loss of provinces, consequently the conquest of them by us.

Here, again, on account of the various significations of these means, so likewise it will be found that neither of them will be identical in its signification in all cases if the objects are different. The smallness in general of this difference must not cause us perplexity, for in reality the weakest motives, the finest shades of difference, often decide in favour of this or that method of applying force. Our only business here is to show that, certain conditions being supposed, the possibility of attaining our purpose in different ways is no contradiction, absurdity, nor even error.

Besides these two means, there are three other peculiar ways of directly increasing the waste of the enemy's force. The first is invasion, that is the occupation of the enemy's territory, not with a view to keeping it, but in order to levy contributions upon it, or to devastate it.

The immediate object here is neither the conquest of the enemy's territory nor the defeat of his armed force, but merely to do him damage in a general way. The second way is to select for the object of our enterprises those points at which we can do the enemy most harm. Nothing is easier to conceive than two different directions in which our force may be employed, the first of which is to be preferred if our object is to defeat the enemy's Army, while the other is more advantageous if the defeat of the enemy is out of the question. According to the usual mode of speaking, we should say that the first is primarily military, the other more political. But if we take our view from the highest point, both are equally military, and neither the one nor the other can be eligible unless it suits the circumstances of the case. The third, by far the most important, from the great number of cases which it embraces, is the wearing out of the enemy. We choose this expression not only to explain our meaning in few words, but because it represents the thing exactly, and is not so figurative as may at first appear. The idea of wearing out in a struggle amounts in practice to a gradual exhaustion of the physical powers and of the will by the long continuance of exertion.

Now, if we want to overcome the enemy by the duration of the contest, we must content ourselves with as small objects as possible, for it is in the nature of the thing that a great end requires a greater expenditure of force than a small one; but the smallest object that we can propose to ourselves is simple passive resistance, that is a combat without any positive view. In this way, therefore, our means attain their greatest relative value, and therefore the result is best secured. How far now can this negative mode of proceeding be carried? Plainly not to absolute passivity, for mere endurance would not be fighting; and the defensive is an activity by which so much of the enemy's power must be destroyed that he must give up his object. That alone is what we aim at in each single act, and therein consists the negative nature of our object.

No doubt this negative object in its single act is not so effective as the positive object in the same direction would be, supposing it successful; but there is this difference in its favour, that it succeeds more easily than the positive, and therefore it holds out greater certainty of success; what is wanting in the efficacy of its single act must be gained through time, that is, through the duration of the contest, and therefore this negative intention, which constitutes the principle of the pure defensive, is also the natural means of overcoming the enemy by the duration of the combat, that is of wearing him out.

Here lies the origin of that difference of Offensive and Defensive, the influence of which prevails throughout the whole province of War. We cannot at present pursue this subject further than to observe that from this negative intention are to be deduced all the advantages and all the stronger forms of combat which are on the side of the Defensive, and in which that philosophical-dynamic law which exists between the greatness and the certainty of success is realised. We shall resume the consideration of all this hereafter.

If then the negative purpose, that is the concentration of all the means into a state of pure resistance, affords a superiority in the contest, and if this advantage is sufficient to balance whatever superiority in numbers the adversary may have, then the mere duration of the contest will suffice gradually to bring the loss of force on the part of the adversary to a point at which the political object can no longer be an equivalent, a point at which, therefore, he must give up the contest. We see then that this class of means, the wearing out of the enemy, includes the great number of cases in which the weaker resists the stronger.

Frederick the Great, during the Seven Years' War, was never strong enough to overthrow the Austrian monarchy; and if he had tried to do so after the fashion of Charles the Twelfth, he would inevitably have had to succumb himself. But after his skilful application of the system of husbanding his resources had shown the powers allied against him, through a seven years' struggle, that the actual expenditure of strength far exceeded what they had at first anticipated, they made peace.

We see then that there are many ways to one's object in War; that the complete subjugation of the enemy is not essential in every case; that the destruction of the enemy's military force, the conquest of the enemy's provinces, the mere occupation of them, the mere invasion of them—enterprises which are aimed directly at political objects—lastly, a passive expectation of the enemy's blow, are all means which, each in itself, may be used to force the enemy's will according as the peculiar circumstances of the case lead us to expect more from the one or the other. We could still add to these a whole category of shorter methods of gaining the end, which might be called arguments ad hominem. What branch of human affairs is there in which these sparks of individual spirit have not made their appearance, surmounting all formal considerations? And least of all can they fail to appear in War, where the personal character of the combatants plays such an important part, both in the cabinet and in the field. We limit ourselves to pointing this out, as it would be pedantry to attempt to reduce such influences into classes. Including these, we may say that the number of possible ways of reaching the object rises to infinity.

To avoid under-estimating these different short roads to one's purpose, either estimating them only as rare exceptions, or holding the difference which they cause in the conduct of War as insignificant, we must bear in mind the diversity of political objects which may cause a War—measure at a glance the distance which there is between a death struggle for political existence and a War which a forced or tottering alliance makes a matter of disagreeable duty. Between the two innumerable gradations occur in practice. If we reject one of these gradations in theory, we might with equal right reject the whole, which would be tantamount to shutting the real world completely out of sight.

These are the circumstances in general connected with the aim which we have to pursue in War; let us now turn to the means.

There is only one single means, it is the Fight. However diversified this may be in form, however widely it may differ from a rough vent of hatred and animosity in a hand-to-hand encounter, whatever number of things may introduce themselves which are not actual fighting, still it is always implied in the conception of War that all the effects manifested have their roots in the combat.

That this must always be so in the greatest diversity and complication of the reality is proved in a very simple manner. All that takes place in War takes place through armed forces, but where the forces of War, i.e., armed men, are applied, there the idea of fighting must of necessity be at the foundation.

All, therefore, that relates to forces of War—all that is connected with their creation, maintenance, and application—belongs to military activity.

Creation and maintenance are obviously only the means, whilst application is the object.

The contest in War is not a contest of individual against individual, but an organised whole, consisting of manifold parts; in this great whole we may distinguish units of two kinds, the one determined by the subject, the other by the object. In an Army the mass of combatants ranges itself always into an order of new units, which again form members of a higher order. The combat of each of these members forms, therefore, also a more or less distinct unit. Further, the motive of the fight; therefore its object forms its unit.

Now, to each of these units which we distinguish in the contest we attach the name of combat.

If the idea of combat lies at the foundation of every application of armed power, then also the application of armed force in general is nothing more than the determining and arranging a certain number of combats.

Every activity in War, therefore, necessarily relates to the combat either directly or indirectly. The soldier is levied, clothed, armed, exercised, he sleeps, eats, drinks, and marches, all merely to fight at the right time and place.

If, therefore, all the threads of military activity terminate in the combat, we shall grasp them all when we settle the order of the combats. Only from this order and its execution proceed the effects, never directly from the conditions preceding them. Now, in the combat all the action is directed to the destruction of the enemy, or rather of his fighting powers, for this lies in the conception of combat. The destruction of the enemy's fighting power is, therefore, always the means to attain the object of the combat.

This object may likewise be the mere destruction of the enemy's armed force; but that is not by any means necessary, and it may be something quite different. Whenever, for instance, as we have shown, the defeat of the enemy is not the only means to attain the political object, whenever there are other objects which may be pursued as the aim in a War, then it follows of itself that such other objects may become the object of particular acts of Warfare, and therefore also the object of combats.

But even those combats which, as subordinate acts, are in the strict sense devoted to the destruction of the enemy's fighting force need not have that destruction itself as their first object.

If we think of the manifold parts of a great armed force, of the number of circumstances which come into activity when it is employed, then it is clear that the combat of such a force must also require a manifold organisation, a subordinating of parts and formation. There may and must naturally arise for particular parts a number of objects which are not themselves the destruction of the enemy's armed force, and which, while they certainly contribute to increase that destruction, do so only in an indirect manner. If a battalion is ordered to drive the enemy from a rising ground, or a bridge, &c., then properly the occupation of any such locality is the real object, the destruction of the enemy's armed force which takes place only the means or secondary matter. If the enemy can be driven away merely by a demonstration, the object is attained all the same; but this hill or bridge is, in point of fact, only required as a means of increasing the gross amount of loss inflicted on the enemy's armed force. It is the case on the field of battle, much more must it be so on the whole theatre of war, where not only one Army is opposed to another, but one State, one Nation, one whole country to another. Here the number of possible relations, and consequently possible combinations, is much greater, the diversity of measures increased, and by the gradation of objects, each subordinate to another the first means employed is further apart from the ultimate object.

It is therefore for many reasons possible that the object of a combat is not the destruction of the enemy's force, that is, of the force immediately opposed to us, but that this only appears as a means. But in all such cases it is no longer a question of complete destruction, for the combat is here nothing else but a measure of strength—has in itself no value except only that of the present result, that is, of its decision.

But a measuring of strength may be effected in cases where the opposing sides are very unequal by a mere comparative estimate. In such cases no fighting will take place, and the weaker will immediately give way.

If the object of a combat is not always the destruction of the enemy's forces therein engaged—and if its object can often be attained as well without the combat taking place at all, by merely making a resolve to fight, and by the circumstances to which this resolution gives rise—then that explains how a whole campaign may be carried on with great activity without the actual combat playing any notable part in it.

That this may be so military history proves by a hundred examples. How many of those cases can be justified, that is, without involving a contradiction and whether some of the celebrities who rose out of them would stand criticism, we shall leave undecided, for all we have to do with the matter is to show the possibility of such a course of events in War.

We have only one means in War—the battle; but this means, by the infinite variety of paths in which it may be applied, leads us into all the different ways which the multiplicity of objects allows of, so that we seem to have gained nothing; but that is not the case, for from this unity of means proceeds a thread which assists the study of the subject, as it runs through the whole web of military activity and holds it together.

But we have considered the destruction of the enemy's force as one of the objects which maybe pursued in War, and left undecided what relative importance should be given to it amongst other objects. In certain cases it will depend on circumstances, and as a general question we have left its value undetermined. We are once more brought back upon it, and we shall be able to get an insight into the value which must necessarily be accorded to it.

The combat is the single activity in War; in the combat the destruction of the enemy opposed to us is the means to the end; it is so even when the combat does not actually take place, because in that case there lies at the root of the decision the supposition at all events that this destruction is to be regarded as beyond doubt. It follows, therefore, that the destruction of the enemy's military force is the foundation-stone of all action in War, the great support of all combinations, which rest upon it like the arch on its abutments. All action, therefore, takes place on the supposition that if the solution by force of arms which lies at its foundation should be realised, it will be a favourable one. The decision by arms is, for all operations in War, great and small, what cash payment is in bill transactions. However remote from each other these relations, however seldom the realisation may take place, still it can never entirely fail to occur.

If the decision by arms lies at the foundation of all combinations, then it follows that the enemy can defeat each of them by gaining a victory on the field, not merely in the one on which our combination directly depends, but also in any other encounter, if it is only important enough; for every important decision by arms—that is, destruction of the enemy's forces—reacts upon all preceding it, because, like a liquid element, they tend to bring themselves to a level.

Thus, the destruction of the enemy's armed force appears, therefore, always as the superior and more effectual means, to which all others must give way.

It is, however, only when there is a supposed equality in all other conditions that we can ascribe to the destruction of the enemy's armed force the greater efficacy. It would, therefore, be a great mistake to draw the conclusion that a blind dash must always gain the victory over skill and caution. An unskilful attack would lead to the destruction of our own and not of the enemy's force, and therefore is not what is here meant. The superior efficacy belongs not to the means but to the end, and we are only comparing the effect of one realised purpose with the other.

If we speak of the destruction of the enemy's armed force, we must expressly point out that nothing obliges us to confine this idea to the mere physical force; on the contrary, the moral is necessarily implied as well, because both in fact are interwoven with each other, even in the most minute details, and therefore cannot be separated. But it is just in connection with the inevitable effect which has been referred to, of a great act of destruction (a great victory) upon all other decisions by arms, that this moral element is most fluid, if we may use that expression, and therefore distributes itself the most easily through all the parts.

Against the far superior worth which the destruction of the enemy's armed force has over all other means stands the expense and risk of this means, and it is only to avoid these that any other means are taken. That these must be costly stands to reason, for the waste of our own military forces must, ceteris paribus, always be greater the more our aim is directed upon the destruction of the enemy's power.

The danger lies in this, that the greater efficacy which we seek recoils on ourselves, and therefore has worse consequences in case we fail of success.

Other methods are, therefore, less costly when they succeed, less dangerous when they fail; but in this is necessarily lodged the condition that they are only opposed to similar ones, that is, that the enemy acts on the same principle; for if the enemy should choose the way of a great decision by arms, our means must on that account be changed against our will, in order to correspond with his. Then all depends on the issue of the act of destruction; but of course it is evident that, ceteris paribus, in this act we must be at a disadvantage in all respects because our views and our means had been directed in part upon other objects, which is not the case with the enemy. Two different objects of which one is not part, the other exclude each other, and therefore a force which may be applicable for the one may not serve for the other. If, therefore, one of two belligerents is determined to seek the great decision by arms, then he has a high probability of success, as soon as he is certain his opponent will not take that way, but follows a different object; and every one who sets before himself any such other aim only does so in a reasonable manner, provided he acts on the supposition that his adversary has as little intention as he has of resorting to the great decision by arms.

But what we have here said of another direction of views and forces relates only to other positive objects, which we may propose to ourselves in War, besides the destruction of the enemy's force, not by any means to the pure defensive, which may be adopted with a view thereby to exhaust the enemy's forces. In the pure defensive the positive object is wanting, and therefore, while on the defensive, our forces cannot at the same time be directed on other objects; they can only be employed to defeat the intentions of the enemy.

We have now to consider the opposite of the destruction of the enemy's armed force, that is to say, the preservation of our own. These two efforts always go together, as they mutually act and react on each other; they are integral parts of one and the same view, and we have only to ascertain what effect is produced when one or the other has the predominance. The endeavour to destroy the enemy's force has a positive object, and leads to positive results, of which the final aim is the conquest of the enemy. The preservation of our own forces has a negative object, leads therefore to the defeat of the enemy's intentions, that is to pure resistance, of which the final aim can be nothing more than to prolong the duration of the contest, so that the enemy shall exhaust himself in it.

The effort with a positive object calls into existence the act of destruction; the effort with the negative object awaits it.

How far this state of expectation should and may be carried we shall enter into more particularly in the theory of attack and defence, at the origin of which we again find ourselves. Here we shall content ourselves with saying that the awaiting must be no absolute endurance, and that in the action bound up with it the destruction of the enemy's armed force engaged in this conflict may be the aim just as well as anything else. It would therefore be a great error in the fundamental idea to suppose that the consequence of the negative course is that we are precluded from choosing the destruction of the enemy's military force as our object, and must prefer a bloodless solution. The advantage which the negative effort gives may certainly lead to that, but only at the risk of its not being the most advisable method, as that question is dependent on totally different conditions, resting not with ourselves but with our opponents. This other bloodless way cannot, therefore, be looked upon at all as the natural means of satisfying our great anxiety to spare our forces; on the contrary, when circumstances are not favourable, it would be the means of completely ruining them. Very many Generals have fallen into this error, and been ruined by it. The only necessary effect resulting from the superiority of the negative effort is the delay of the decision, so that the party acting takes refuge in that way, as it were, in the expectation of the decisive moment. The consequence of that is generally the postponement of the action as much as possible in time, and also in space, in so far as space is in connection with it. If the moment has arrived in which this can no longer be done without ruinous disadvantage, then the advantage of the negative must be considered as exhausted, and then comes forward unchanged the effort for the destruction of the enemy's force, which was kept back by a counterpoise, but never discarded.

We have seen, therefore, in the foregoing reflections, that there are many ways to the aim, that is, to the attainment of the political object; but that the only means is the combat, and that consequently everything is subject to a supreme law: which is the decision by arms; that where this is really demanded by one, it is a redress which cannot be refused by the other; that, therefore, a belligerent who takes any other way must make sure that his opponent will not take this means of redress, or his cause may be lost in that supreme court; hence therefore the destruction of the enemy's armed force, amongst all the objects which can be pursued in War, appears always as the one which overrules all others.

What may be achieved by combinations of another kind in War we shall only learn in the sequel, and naturally only by degrees. We content ourselves here with acknowledging in general their possibility, as something pointing to the difference between the reality and the conception, and to the influence of particular circumstances. But we could not avoid showing at once that the bloody solution of the crisis, the effort for the destruction of the enemy's force, is the firstborn son of War. If when political objects are unimportant, motives weak, the excitement of forces small, a cautious commander tries in all kinds of ways, without great crises and bloody solutions, to twist himself skilfully into a peace through the characteristic weaknesses of his enemy in the field and in the Cabinet, we have no right to find fault with him, if the premises on which he acts are well founded and justified by success; still we must require him to remember that he only travels on forbidden tracks, where the God of War may surprise him; that he ought always to keep his eye on the enemy, in order that he may not have to defend himself with a dress rapier if the enemy takes up a sharp sword.

The consequences of the nature of War, how ends and means act in it, how in the modifications of reality it deviates sometimes more, sometimes less, from its strict original conception, fluctuating backwards and forwards, yet always remaining under that strict conception as under a supreme law: all this we must retain before us, and bear constantly in mind in the consideration of each of the succeeding subjects, if we would rightly comprehend their true relations and proper importance, and not become involved incessantly in the most glaring contradictions with the reality, and at last with our own selves.

CHAPTER III. The Genius for War

Every special calling in life, if it is to be followed with success, requires peculiar qualifications of understanding and soul. Where these are of a high order, and manifest themselves by extraordinary achievements, the mind to which they belong is termed GENIUS.

We know very well that this word is used in many significations which are very different both in extent and nature, and that with many of these significations it is a very difficult task to define the essence of Genius; but as we neither profess to be philosopher nor grammarian, we must be allowed to keep to the meaning usual in ordinary language, and to understand by "genius" a very high mental capacity for certain employments.

We wish to stop for a moment over this faculty and dignity of the mind, in order to vindicate its title, and to explain more fully the meaning of the conception. But we shall not dwell on that (genius) which has obtained its title through a very great talent, on genius properly so called, that is a conception which has no defined limits. What we have to do is to bring under consideration every common tendency of the powers of the mind and soul towards the business of War, the whole of which common tendencies we may look upon as the ESSENCE OF MILITARY GENIUS. We say "common," for just therein consists military genius, that it is not one single quality bearing upon War, as, for instance, courage, while other qualities of mind and soul are wanting or have a direction which is unserviceable for War, but that it is AN HARMONIOUS ASSOCIATION OF POWERS, in which one or other may predominate, but none must be in opposition.

If every combatant required to be more or less endowed with military genius, then our armies would be very weak; for as it implies a peculiar bent of the intelligent powers, therefore it can only rarely be found where the mental powers of a people are called into requisition and trained in many different ways. The fewer the employments followed by a Nation, the more that of arms predominates, so much the more prevalent will military genius also be found. But this merely applies to its prevalence, by no means to its degree, for that depends on the general state of intellectual culture in the country. If we look at a wild, warlike race, then we find a warlike spirit in individuals much more common than in a civilised people; for in the former almost every warrior possesses it, whilst in the civilised whole, masses are only carried away by it from necessity, never by inclination. But amongst uncivilised people we never find a really great General, and very seldom what we can properly call a military genius, because that requires a development of the intelligent powers which cannot be found in an uncivilised state. That a civilised people may also have a warlike tendency and development is a matter of course; and the more this is general, the more frequently also will military spirit be found in individuals in their armies. Now as this coincides in such case with the higher degree of civilisation, therefore from such nations have issued forth the most brilliant military exploits, as the Romans and the French have exemplified. The greatest names in these and in all other nations that have been renowned in War belong strictly to epochs of higher culture.

From this we may infer how great a share the intelligent powers have in superior military genius. We shall now look more closely into this point.

War is the province of danger, and therefore courage above all things is the first quality of a warrior.

Courage is of two kinds: first, physical courage, or courage in presence of danger to the person; and next, moral courage, or courage before responsibility, whether it be before the judgment-seat of external authority, or of the inner power, the conscience. We only speak here of the first.

Courage before danger to the person, again, is of two kinds. First, it may be indifference to danger, whether proceeding from the organism of the individual, contempt of death, or habit: in any of these cases it is to be regarded as a permanent condition.

Secondly, courage may proceed from positive motives, such as personal pride, patriotism, enthusiasm of any kind. In this case courage is not so much a normal condition as an impulse.

We may conceive that the two kinds act differently. The first kind is more certain, because it has become a second nature, never forsakes the man; the second often leads him farther. In the first there is more of firmness, in the second, of boldness. The first leaves the judgment cooler, the second raises its power at times, but often bewilders it. The two combined make up the most perfect kind of courage.

War is the province of physical exertion and suffering. In order not to be completely overcome by them, a certain strength of body and mind is required, which, either natural or acquired, produces indifference to them. With these qualifications, under the guidance of simply a sound understanding, a man is at once a proper instrument for War; and these are the qualifications so generally to be met with amongst wild and half-civilised tribes. If we go further in the demands which War makes on it, then we find the powers of the understanding predominating. War is the province of uncertainty: three-fourths of those things upon which action in War must be calculated, are hidden more or less in the clouds of great uncertainty. Here, then, above all a fine and penetrating mind is called for, to search out the truth by the tact of its judgment.

An average intellect may, at one time, perhaps hit upon this truth by accident; an extraordinary courage, at another, may compensate for the want of this tact; but in the majority of cases the average result will always bring to light the deficient understanding.

War is the province of chance. In no sphere of human activity is such a margin to be left for this intruder, because none is so much in constant contact with him on all sides. He increases the uncertainty of every circumstance, and deranges the course of events.

From this uncertainty of all intelligence and suppositions, this continual interposition of chance, the actor in War constantly finds things different from his expectations; and this cannot fail to have an influence on his plans, or at least on the presumptions connected with these plans. If this influence is so great as to render the pre-determined plan completely nugatory, then, as a rule, a new one must be substituted in its place; but at the moment the necessary data are often wanting for this, because in the course of action circumstances press for immediate decision, and allow no time to look about for fresh data, often not enough for mature consideration.

But it more often happens that the correction of one premise, and the knowledge of chance events which have arisen, are not sufficient to overthrow our plans completely, but only suffice to produce hesitation. Our knowledge of circumstances has increased, but our uncertainty, instead of having diminished, has only increased. The reason of this is, that we do not gain all our experience at once, but by degrees; thus our determinations continue to be assailed incessantly by fresh experience; and the mind, if we may use the expression, must always be “under arms.”

Now, if it is to get safely through this perpetual conflict with the unexpected, two qualities are indispensable: in the first place an intellect which, even in the midst of this intense obscurity, is not without some traces of inner light, which lead to the truth, and then the courage to follow this faint light. The first is figuratively expressed by the French phrase coup d’œil. The other is resolution. As the battle is the feature in War to which attention was originally chiefly directed, and as time and space are important elements in it, more particularly when cavalry with their rapid decisions were the chief arm, the idea of rapid and correct decision related in the first instance to the estimation of these two elements, and to denote the idea an expression was adopted which actually only points to a correct judgment by eye. Many teachers of the Art of War then gave this limited signification as the definition of coup d’œil. But it is undeniable that all able decisions formed in the moment of action soon came to be understood by the expression, as, for instance, the hitting upon the right point of attack, &c. It is, therefore, not only the physical, but more frequently the mental eye which is meant in coup d’œil. Naturally, the expression, like the thing, is always more in its place in the field of tactics: still, it must not be wanting in strategy, inasmuch as in it rapid decisions are often necessary. If we strip this conception of that which the expression has given it of the over-figurative and restricted, then it amounts simply to the rapid discovery of a truth which to the ordinary mind is either not visible at all or only becomes so after long examination and reflection.

Resolution is an act of courage in single instances, and if it becomes a characteristic trait, it is a habit of the mind. But here we do not mean courage in face of bodily danger, but in face of responsibility, therefore, to a certain extent against moral danger. This has been often called courage d'esprit, on the ground that it springs from the understanding; nevertheless, it is no act of the understanding on that account; it is an act of feeling. Mere intelligence is still not courage, for we often see the cleverest people devoid of resolution. The mind must, therefore, first awaken the feeling of courage, and then be guided and supported by it, because in momentary emergencies the man is swayed more by his feelings than his thoughts.

We have assigned to resolution the office of removing the torments of doubt, and the dangers of delay, when there are no sufficient motives for guidance. Through the unscrupulous use of language which is prevalent, this term is often applied to the mere propensity to daring, to bravery, boldness, or temerity. But, when there are sufficient motives in the man, let them be objective or subjective, true or false, we have no right to speak of his resolution; for, when we do so, we put ourselves in his place, and we throw into the scale doubts which did not exist with him.

Here there is no question of anything but of strength and weakness. We are not pedantic enough to dispute with the use of language about this little misapplication, our observation is only intended to remove wrong objections.

This resolution now, which overcomes the state of doubting, can only be called forth by the intellect, and, in fact, by a peculiar tendency of the same. We maintain that the mere union of a superior understanding and the necessary feelings are not sufficient to make up resolution. There are persons who possess the keenest perception for the most difficult problems, who are also not fearful of responsibility, and yet in cases of difficulty cannot come to a resolution. Their courage and their sagacity operate independently of each other, do not give each other a hand, and on that account do not produce resolution as a result. The forerunner of resolution is an act of the mind making evident the necessity of venturing, and thus influencing the will. This quite peculiar direction of the mind, which conquers every other fear in man by the fear of wavering or doubting, is what makes up resolution in strong minds; therefore, in our opinion, men who have little intelligence can never be resolute. They may act without hesitation under perplexing circumstances, but then they act without reflection. Now, of course, when a man acts without reflection he cannot be at variance with himself by doubts, and such a mode of action may now and then lead to the right point; but we say now as before, it is the average result which indicates the existence of military genius. Should our assertion appear extraordinary to any one, because he knows many a resolute hussar officer who is no deep thinker, we must remind him that the question here is about a peculiar direction of the mind, and not about great thinking powers.

We believe, therefore, that resolution is indebted to a special direction of the mind for its existence, a direction which belongs to a strong head rather than to a brilliant one. In corroboration of this genealogy of resolution we may add that there have been many instances of men who have shown the greatest resolution in an inferior rank, and have lost it in a higher position. While, on the one hand, they are obliged to resolve, on the other they see the dangers of a wrong decision, and as they are surrounded with things new to them, their understanding loses its original forcc, and they become only the more timid the more they become aware of the danger of the irresolution into which they have fallen, and the more they have formerly been in the habit of acting on the spur of the moment.

From the coup d'œil and resolution we are naturally to speak of its kindred quality, presence of mind, which in a region of the unexpected like War must act a great part, for it is indeed nothing but a great conquest over the unexpected. As we admire presence of mind in a pithy answer to anything said unexpectedly, so we admire it in a ready expedient on sudden danger. Neither the answer nor the expedient need be in themselves extraordinary, if they only hit the point; for that which as the result of mature reflection would be nothing unusual, therefore insignificant in its impression on us, may as an instantaneous act of the mind produce a pleasing impression. The expression "presence of mind" certainly denotes very fitly the readiness and rapidity of the help rendered by the mind.

Whether this noble quality of a man is to be ascribed more to the peculiarity of his mind or to the equanimity of his feelings, depends on the nature of the case, although neither of the two can be entirely wanting. A telling repartee bespeaks rather a ready wit, a ready expedient on sudden danger implies more particularly a well-balanced mind.

If we take a general view of the four elements composing the atmosphere in which War moves, of danger, physical effort, uncertainty, and chance, it is easy to conceive that a great force of mind and understanding is requisite to be able to make way with safety and success amongst such opposing elements, a force which, according to the different modifications arising out of circumstances, we find termed by military writers and annalists as energy, firmness, staunchness, strength of mind and character. All these manifestations of the heroic nature might be regarded as one and the same power of volition, modified according to circumstances; but nearly related as these things are to each other, still they are not one and the same, and it is desirable for us to distinguish here a little more closely at least the action of the powers of the soul in relation to them.

In the first place, to make the conception clear, it is essential to observe that the weight, burden, resistance, or whatever it may be called, by which that force of the soul in the General is brought to light, is only in a very small measure the enemy's activity, the enemy's resistance, the enemy's action directly. The enemy's activity only affects the General directly in the first place in relation to his person, without disturbing his action as Commander. If the enemy, instead of two hours, resists for four, the Commander instead of two hours is four hours in danger; this is a quantity which plainly diminishes the higher the rank of the Commander. What is it for one in the post of Commander-in-Chief? It is nothing.

Secondly, although the opposition offered by the enemy has a direct effect on the Commander through the loss of means arising from prolonged resistance, and the responsibility connected with that loss, and his force of will is first tested and called forth by these anxious considerations, still we maintain that this is not the heaviest burden by far which he has to bear, because he has only himself to settle with. All the other effects of the enemy's resistance act directly upon the combatants under his command, and through them react upon him.

As long as his men full of good courage fight with zeal and spirit, it is seldom necessary for the Chief to show great energy of purpose in the pursuit of his object. But as soon as difficulties arise—and that must always happen when great results are at stake—then things no longer move on of themselves like a well-oiled machine, the machine itself then begins to offer resistance, and to overcome this the Commander must have a great force of will. By this resistance we must not exactly suppose disobedience and murmurs, although these are frequent enough with particular individuals; it is the whole feeling of the dissolution of all physical and moral power, it is the heartrending sight of the bloody sacrifice which the Commander has to contend with in himself, and then in all others who directly or indirectly transfer to him their impressions, feelings, anxieties, and desires. As the forces in one individual after another become prostrated, and can no longer be excited and supported by an effort of his own will, the whole inertia of the mass gradually rests its weight on the Will of the Commander: by the spark in his breast, by the light of his spirit, the spark of purpose, the light of hope, must be kindled afresh in others: in so far only as he is equal to this, he stands above the masses and continues to be their master; whenever that influence ceases, and his own spirit is no longer strong enough to revive the spirit of all others, the masses drawing him down with them sink into the lower region of animal nature, which shrinks from danger and knows not shame. These are the weights which the courage and intelligent faculties of the military Commander have to overcome if he is to make his name illustrious. They increase with the masses, and therefore, if the forces in question are to continue equal to the burden, they must rise in proportion to the height of the station.

Energy in action expresses the strength of the motive through which the action is excited, let the motive have its origin in a conviction of the understanding, or in an impulse. But the latter can hardly ever be wanting where great force is to show itself.

Of all the noble feelings which fill the human heart in the exciting tumult of battle, none, we must admit, are so powerful and constant as the soul's thirst for honour and renown, which the German language treats so unfairly and tends to depreciate by the unworthy associations in the words Ehrgeiz (greed of honour) and Ruhmsucht (hankering after glory). No doubt it is just in War that the abuse of these proud aspirations of the soul must bring upon the human race the most shocking outrages, but by their origin they are certainly to be counted amongst the noblest feelings which belong to human nature, and in War they are the vivifying principle which gives the enormous body a spirit. Although other feelings may be more general in their influence, and many of them—such as love of country, fanaticism, revenge, enthusiasm of every kind—may seem to stand higher, the thirst for honour and renown still remains indispensable. Those other feelings may rouse the great masses in general, and excite them more powerfully, but they do not give the Leader a desire to will more than others, which is an essential requisite in his position if he is to make himself distinguished in it. They do not, like a thirst for honour, make the military act specially the property of the Leader, which he strives to turn to the best account; where he ploughs with toil, sows with care, that he may reap plentifully. It is through these aspirations we have been speaking of in Commanders, from the highest to the lowest, this sort of energy, this spirit of emulation, these incentives, that the action of armies is chiefly animated and made successful. And now as to that which specially concerns the head of all, we ask, Has there ever been a great Commander destitute of the love of honour, or is such a character even conceivable?

Firmness denotes the resistance of the will in relation to the force of a single blow, staunchness in relation to a continuance of blows. Close as is the analogy between the two, and often as the one is used in place of the other, still there is a notable difference between them which cannot be mistaken, inasmuch as firmness against a single powerful impression may have its root in the mere strength of a feeling, but staunchness must be supported rather by the understanding, for the greater the duration of an action the more systematic deliberation is connected with it, and from this staunchness partly derives its power.

If we now turn to strength of mind or soul, then the first question is, What are we to understand thereby?

Plainly it is not vehement expressions of feeling, nor easily excited passions, for that would be contrary to all the usage of language, but the power of listening to reason in the midst of the most intense excitement, in the storm of the most violent passions. Should this power depend on strength of understanding alone? We doubt it. The fact that there are men of the greatest intellect who cannot command themselves certainly proves nothing to the contrary, for we might say that it perhaps requires an understanding of a powerful rather than of a comprehensive nature; but we believe we shall be nearer the truth if we assume that the power of submitting oneself to the control of the understanding, even in moments of the most violent excitement of the feelings, that power which we call self-command, has its root in the heart itself. It is, in point of fact, another feeling, which in strong minds balances the excited passions without destroying them; and it is only through this equilibrium that the mastery of the understanding is secured. This counterpoise is nothing but a sense of the dignity of man, that noblest pride, that deeply-seated desire of the soul always to act as a being endued with understanding and reason. We may therefore say that a strong mind is one which does not lose its balance even under the most violent excitement.

If we cast a glance at the variety to be observed in the human character in respect to feeling, we find, first, some people who have very little excitability, who are called phlegmatic or indolent.

Secondly, some very excitable, but whose feelings still never overstep certain limits, and who are therefore known as men full of feeling, but sober-minded.

Thirdly, those who are very easily roused, whose feelings blaze up quickly and violently like gunpowder, but do not last.

Fourthly, and lastly, those who cannot be moved by slight causes, and who generally are not to be roused suddenly, but only gradually; but whose feelings become very powerful and are much more lasting. These are men with strong passions, lying deep and latent.

This difference of character lies probably close on the confines of the physical powers which move the human organism, and belongs to that amphibious organisation which we call the nervous system, which appears to be partly material, partly spiritual. With our weak philosophy, we shall not proceed further in this mysterious field. But it is important for us to spend a moment over the effects which these different natures have on, action in War, and to see how far a great strength of mind is to be expected from them.

Indolent men cannot easily be thrown out of their equanimity, but we cannot certainly say there is strength of mind where there is a want of all manifestation of power.

At the same time, it is not to be denied that such men have a certain peculiar aptitude for War, on account of their constant equanimity. They often want the positive motive to action, impulse, and consequently activity, but they are not apt to throw things into disorder.

The peculiarity of the second class is that they are easily excited to act on trifling grounds, but in great matters they are easily overwhelmed. Men of this kind show great activity in helping an unfortunate individual, but by the distress of a whole Nation they are only inclined to despond, not roused to action.

Such people are not deficient in either activity or equanimity in War; but they will never accomplish anything great unless a great intellectual force furnishes the motive, and it is very seldom that a strong, independent mind is combined with such a character.

Excitable, inflammable feelings are in themselves little suited for practical life, and therefore they are not very fit for War. They have certainly the advantage of strong impulses, but that cannot long sustain them. At the same time, if the excitability in such men takes the direction of courage, or a sense of honour, they may often be very useful in inferior positions in War, because the action in War over which commanders in inferior positions have control is generally of shorter duration. Here one courageous resolution, one effervescence of the forces of the soul, will often suffice. A brave attack, a soul-stirring hurrah, is the work of a few moments, whilst a brave contest on the battle-field is the work of a day, and a campaign the work of a year.

Owing to the rapid movement of their feelings, it is doubly difficult for men of this description to preserve equilibrium of the mind; therefore they frequently lose head, and that is the worst phase in their nature as respects the conduct of War. But it would be contrary to experience to maintain that very excitable spirits can never preserve a steady equilibrium—that is to say, that they cannot do so even under the strongest excitement. Why should they not have the sentiment of self-respect, for, as a rule, they are men of a noble nature? This feeling is seldom wanting in them, but it has not time to produce an effect. After an outburst they suffer most from a feeling of inward humiliation. If through education, self-observance, and experience of life, they have learned, sooner or later, the means of being on their guard, so that at the moment of powerful excitement they are conscious betimes of the counteracting force within their own breasts, then even such men may have great strength of mind.

Lastly, those who are difficult to move, but on that account susceptible of very deep feelings, men who stand in the same relation to the preceding as red heat to a flame, are the best adapted by means of their Titanic strength to roll away the enormous masses by which we may figuratively represent the difficulties which beset command in War. The effect of their feelings is like the movement of a great body, slower, but more irresistible.

Although such men are not so likely to be suddenly surprised by their feelings and carried away so as to be afterwards ashamed of themselves, like the preceding, still it would be contrary to experience to believe that they can never lose their equanimity, or be overcome by blind passion; on the contrary, this must always happen whenever the noble pride of self-control is wanting, or as often as it has not sufficient weight. We see examples of this most frequently in men of noble minds belonging to savage nations, where the low degree of mental cultivation favours always the dominance of the passions. But even amongst the most civilised classes in civilised States, life is full of examples of this kind—of men carried away by the violence of their passions, like the poacher of old chained to the stag in the forest.

We therefore say once more a strong mind is not one that is merely susceptible of strong excitement, but one which can maintain its serenity under the most powerful excitement, so that, in spite of the storm in the breast, the perception and judgment can act with perfect freedom, like the needle of the compass in the storm-tossed ship.

By the term strength of character, or simply character, is denoted tenacity of conviction, let it be the result of our own or of others' views, and whether they are principles, opinions, momentary inspirations, or any kind of emanations of the understanding; but this kind of firmness certainly cannot manifest itself if the views themselves are subject to frequent change. This frequent change need not be the consequence of external influences; it may proceed from the continuous activity of our own mind, in which case it indicates a characteristic unsteadiness of mind. Evidently we should not say of a man who changes his views every moment, however much the motives of change may originate with himself, that he has character. Only those men, therefore, can be said to have this quality whose conviction is very constant, either because it is deeply rooted and clear in itself, little liable to alteration, or because, as in the case of indolent men, there is a want of mental activity, and therefore a want of motives to change; or lastly, because an explicit act of the will, derived from an imperative maxim of the understanding, refuses any change of opinion up to a certain point.

Now in War, owing to the many and powerful impressions to which the mind is exposed, and in the uncertainty of all knowledge and of all science, more things occur to distract a man from the road he has entered upon, to make him doubt himself and others, than in any other human activity.

The harrowing sight of danger and suffering easily leads to the feelings gaining ascendency over the conviction of the understanding; and in the twilight which surrounds everything a deep clear view is so difficult that a change of opinion is more conceivable and more pardonable. It is, at all times, only conjecture or guesses at truth which we have to act upon. This is why differences of opinion are nowhere so great as in War, and the stream of impressions acting counter to one's own convictions never ceases to flow. Even the greatest impassibility of mind is hardly proof against them, because the impressions are powerful in their nature, and always act at the same time upon the feelings.

When the discernment is clear and deep, none but general principles and views of action from a high standpoint can be the result; and on these principles the opinion in each particular case immediately under consideration lies, as it were, at anchor. But to keep to these results of bygone reflection, in opposition to the stream of opinions and phenomena which the present brings with it, is just the difficulty. Between the particular case and the principle there is often a wide space which cannot always be traversed on a visible chain of conclusions, and where a certain faith in self is necessary and a certain amount of scepticism is serviceable. Here often nothing else will help us but an imperative maxim which, independent of reflection, at once controls it: that maxim is, in all doubtful cases to adhere to the first opinion, and not to give it up until a clear conviction forces us to do so. We must firmly believe in the superior authority of well-tried maxims, and under the dazzling influence of momentary events not forget that their value is of an inferior stamp. By this preference which in doubtful cases we give to first convictions, by adherence to the same our actions acquire that stability and consistency which make up what is called character.

It is easy to see how essential a well-balanced mind is to strength of character; therefore men of strong minds generally have a great deal of character.

Force of character leads us to a spurious variety of it—OBSTINACY.

It is often very difficult in concrete cases to say where the one ends and the other begins; on the other hand, it does not seem difficult to determine the difference in idea.

Obstinacy is no fault of the understanding; we use the term as denoting a resistance against our better judgment, and it would be inconsistent to charge that to the understanding, as the understanding is the power of judgment. Obstinacy is A FAULT OF THE FEELINGS or heart. This inflexibility of will, this impatience of contradiction, have their origin only in a particular kind of egotism, which sets above every other pleasure that of governing both self and others by its own mind alone. We should call it a kind of vanity, were it not decidedly something better. Vanity is satisfied with mere show, but obstinacy rests upon the enjoyment of the thing.

We say, therefore, force of character degenerates into obstinacy whenever the resistance to opposing judgments proceeds not from better convictions or a reliance upon a trustworthy maxim, but from a feeling of opposition. If this definition, as we have already admitted, is of little assistance practically, still it will prevent obstinacy from being considered merely force of character intensified, whilst it is something essentially different—something which certainly lies close to it and is cognate to it, but is at the same time so little an intensification of it that there are very obstinate men who from want of understanding have very little force of character.

Having in these high attributes of a great military Commander made ourselves acquainted with those qualities in which heart and head co-operate, we now come to a speciality of military activity which perhaps may be looked upon as the most marked if it is not the most important, and which only makes a demand on the power of the mind without regard to the forces of feelings. It is the connection which exists between War and country or ground.

This connection is, in the first place, a permanent condition of War, for it is impossible to imagine our organised Armies effecting any operation otherwise than in some given space; it is, secondly, of the most decisive importance, because it modifies, at times completely alters, the action of all forces; thirdly, while on the one hand it often concerns the most minute features of locality, on the other it may apply to immense tracts of country.

In this manner a great peculiarity is given to the effect of this connection of War with country and ground. If we think of other occupations of man which have a relation to these objects, on horticulture, agriculture, on building houses and hydraulic works, on mining, on the chase, and forestry, they are all confined within very limited spaces which may be soon explored with sufficient exactness. But the Commander in War must commit the business he has in hand to a corresponding space which his eye cannot survey, which the keenest zeal cannot always explore, and with which, owing to the constant changes taking place, he can also seldom become properly acquainted. Certainly the enemy generally is in the same situation; still, in the first place, the difficulty, although common to both, is not the less a difficulty, and he who by talent and practice overcomes it will have a great advantage on his side; secondly, this equality of the difficulty on both sides is merely an abstract supposition which is rarely realised in the particular case, as one of the two opponents (the defensive) usually knows much more of the locality than his adversary.

This very peculiar difficulty must be overcome by a natural mental gift of a special kind which is known by the—too restricted—term of Ortsinn sense of locality. It is the power of quickly forming a correct geometrical idea of any portion of country, and consequently of being able to find one's place in it exactly at any time. This is plainly an act of the imagination. The perception no doubt is formed partly by means of the physical eye, partly by the mind, which fills up what is wanting with ideas derived from knowledge and experience, and out of the fragments visible to the physical eye forms a whole; but that this whole should present itself vividly to the reason, should become a picture, a mentally drawn map, that this picture should be fixed, that the details should never again separate themselves—all that can only be effected by the mental faculty which we call imagination. If some great poet or painter should feel hurt that we require from his goddess such an office; if he shrugs his shoulders at the notion that a sharp gamekeeper must necessarily excel in imagination, we readily grant that we only speak here of imagination in a limited sense, of its service in a really menial capacity. But, however slight this service, still it must be the work of that natural gift, for if that gift is wanting, it would be difficult to imagine things plainly in all the completeness of the visible. That a good memory is a great assistance we freely allow, but whether memory is to be considered as an independent faculty of the mind in this case, or whether it is just that power of imagination which here fixes these things better on the memory, we leave undecided, as in many respects it seems difficult upon the whole to conceive these two mental powers apart from each other.

That practice and mental acuteness have much to do with it is not to be denied. Puysegur, the celebrated Quartermaster-General of the famous Luxemburg, used to say that he had very little confidence in himself in this respect at first, because if he had to fetch the parole from a distance he always lost his way.

It is natural that scope for the exercise of this talent should increase along with rank. If the hussar and rifleman in command of a patrol must know well all the highways and byways, and if for that a few marks, a few limited powers of observation, are sufficient, the Chief of an Army must make himself familiar with the general geographical features of a province and of a country; must always have vividly before his eyes the direction of the roads, rivers, and hills, without at the same time being able to dispense with the narrower "sense of locality" (Ortsinn). No doubt, information of various kinds as to objects in general, maps, books, memoirs, and for details the assistance of his Staff, are a great help to him; but it is nevertheless certain that if he has himself a talent for forming an ideal picture of a country quickly and distinctly, it lends to his action an easier and firmer step, saves him from a certain mental helplessness, and makes him less dependent on others.

If this talent then is to be ascribed to imagination, it is also almost the only service which military activity requires from that erratic goddess, whose influence is more hurtful than useful in other respects.

We think we have now passed in review those manifestations of the powers of mind and soul which military activity requires from human nature. Everywhere intellect appears as an essential co-operative force; and thus we can understand how the work of War, although so plain and simple in its effects, can never be conducted with distinguished success by people without distinguished powers of the understanding.

When we have reached this view, then we need no longer look upon such a natural idea as the turning an enemy's position, which has been done a thousand times, and a hundred other similar conceptions, as the result of a great effort of genius.

Certainly one is accustomed to regard the plain honest soldier as the very opposite of the man of reflection, full of inventions and ideas, or of the brilliant spirit shining in the ornaments of refined education of every kind. This antithesis is also by no means devoid of truth; but it does not show that the efficiency of the soldier consists only in his courage, and that there is no particular energy and capacity of the brain required in addition to make a man merely what is called a true soldier. We must again repeat that there is nothing more common than to hear of men losing their energy on being raised to a higher position, to which they do not feel themselves equal; but we must also remind our readers that we are speaking of pre-eminent services, of such as give renown in the branch of activity to which they belong. Each grade of command in War therefore forms its own stratum of requisite capacity of fame and honour.

An immense space lies between a General—that is, one at the head of a whole War, or of a theatre of War—and his Second in Command, for the simple reason that the latter is in more immediate subordination to a superior authority and supervision, consequently is restricted to a more limited sphere of independent thought. This is why common opinion sees no room for the exercise of high talent except in high places, and looks upon an ordinary capacity as sufficient for all beneath: this is why people are rather inclined to look upon a subordinate General grown grey in the service, and in whom constant discharge of routine duties has produced a decided poverty of mind, as a man of failing intellect, and, with all respect for his bravery, to laugh at his simplicity. It is not our object to gain for these brave men a better lot—that would contribute nothing to their efficiency, and little to their happiness; we only wish to represent things as they are, and to expose the error of believing that a mere bravo without intellect can make himself distinguished in War.

As we consider distinguished talents requisite for those who are to attain distinction, even in inferior positions, it naturally follows that we think highly of those who fill with renown the place of Second in Command of an Army; and their seeming simplicity of character as compared with a polyhistor, with ready men of business, or with councillors of state, must not lead us astray as to the superior nature of their intellectual activity. It happens sometimes that men import the fame gained in an inferior position into a higher one, without in reality deserving it in the new position; and then if they are not much employed, and therefore not much exposed to the risk of showing their weak points, the judgment does not distinguish very exactly what degree of fame is really due to them; and thus such men are often the occasion of too low an estimate being formed of the characteristics required to shine in certain situations.

For each station, from the lowest upwards, to render distinguished services in War, there must be a particular genius. But the title of genius, history and the judgment of posterity only confer, in general, on those minds which have shone in the highest rank, that of Commanders-in-Chief. The reason is that here, in point of fact, the demand on the reasoning and intellectual powers generally is much greater.

To conduct a whole War, or its great acts, which we call campaigns, to a successful termination, there must be an intimate knowledge of State policy in its higher relations. The conduct of the War and the policy of the State here coincide, and the General becomes at the same time the Statesman.

We do not give Charles XII. the name of a great genius, because he could not make the power of his sword subservient to a higher judgment and philosophy—could not attain by it to a glorious object. We do not give that title to Henry IV. (of France), because he did not live long enough to set at rest the relations of different States by his military activity, and to occupy himself in that higher field where noble feelings and a chivalrous disposition have less to do in mastering the enemy than in overcoming internal dissension.

In order that the reader may appreciate all that must be comprehended and judged of correctly at a glance by a General, we refer to the first chapter. We say the General becomes a Statesman, but he must not cease to be the General. He takes into view all the relations of the State on the one hand; on the other, he must know exactly what he can do with the means at his disposal.

As the diversity, and undefined limits, of all the circumstances bring a great number of factors into consideration in War, as the most of these factors can only be estimated according to probability, therefore, if the Chief of an Army does not bring to bear upon them a mind with an intuitive perception of the truth, a confusion of ideas and views must take place, in the midst of which the judgment will become bewildered. In this sense, Buonaparte was right when he said that many of the questions which come before a General for decision would make problems for a mathematical calculation not unworthy of the powers of Newton or Euler.

What is here required from the higher powers of the mind is a sense of unity, and a judgment raised to such a compass as to give the mind an extraordinary faculty of vision which in its range allays and sets aside a thousand dim notions which an ordinary understanding could only bring to light with great effort, and over which it would exhaust itself. But this higher activity of the mind, this glance of genius, would still not become matter of history if the qualities of temperament and character of which we have treated did not give it their support.

Truth alone is but a weak motive of action with men, and hence there is always a great difference between knowing and action, between science and art. The man receives the strongest impulse to action through the feelings, and the most powerful succour, if we may use the expression, through those faculties of heart and mind which we have considered under the terms of resolution, firmness, perseverance, and force of character.

If, however, this elevated condition of heart and mind in the General did not manifest itself in the general effects resulting from it, and could only be accepted on trust and faith, then it would rarely become matter of history.

All that becomes known of the course of events in War is usually very simple, and has a great sameness in appearance; no one on the mere relation of such events perceives the difficulties connected with them which had to be overcome. It is only now and again, in the memoirs of Generals or of those in their confidence, or by reason of some special historical inquiry directed to a particular circumstance, that a portion of the many threads composing the whole web is brought to light. The reflections, mental doubts, and conflicts which precede the execution of great acts are purposely concealed because they affect political interests, or the recollection of them is accidentally lost because they have been looked upon as mere scaffolding which had to be removed on the completion of the building.

If, now, in conclusion, without venturing upon a closer definition of the higher powers of the soul, we should admit a distinction in the intelligent faculties themselves according to the common ideas established by language, and ask ourselves what kind of mind comes closest to military genius, then a look at the subject as well as at experience will tell us that searching rather than inventive minds, comprehensive minds rather than such as have a special bent, cool rather than fiery heads, are those to which in time of War we should prefer to trust the welfare of our women and children, the honour and the safety of our fatherland.

CHAPTER IV. Of Danger in War

Usually before we have learnt what danger really is, we form an idea of it which is rather attractive than repulsive. In the intoxication of enthusiasm, to fall upon the enemy at the charge—who cares then about bullets and men falling? To throw oneself, blinded by excitement for a moment, against cold death, uncertain whether we or another shall escape him, and all this close to the golden gate of victory, close to the rich fruit which ambition thirsts for—can this be difficult? It will not be difficult, and still less will it appear so. But such moments, which, however, are not the work of a single pulse-beat, as is supposed, but rather like doctors' draughts, must be taken diluted and spoilt by mixture with time—such moments, we say, are but few.

Let us accompany the novice to the battle-field. As we approach, the thunder of the cannon becoming plainer and plainer is soon followed by the howling of shot, which attracts the attention of the inexperienced. Balls begin to strike the ground close to us, before and behind. We hasten to the hill where stands the General and his numerous Staff. Here the close striking of the cannon balls and the bursting of shells is so frequent that the seriousness of life makes itself visible through the youthful picture of imagination. Suddenly some one known to us falls—a shell strikes amongst the crowd and causes some involuntary movements—we begin to feel that we are no longer perfectly at ease and collected; even the bravest is at least to some degree confused. Now, a step farther into the battle which is raging before us like a scene in a theatre, we get to the nearest General of Division; here ball follows ball, and the noise of our own guns increases the confusion. From the General of Division to the Brigadier. He, a man of acknowledged bravery, keeps carefully behind a rising ground, a house, or a tree—a sure sign of increasing danger. Grape rattles on the roofs of the houses and in the fields; cannon balls howl over us, and plough the air in all directions, and soon there is a frequent whistling of musket balls. A step farther towards the troops, to that sturdy infantry which for hours has maintained its firmness under this heavy fire; here the air is filled with the hissing of balls which announce their proximity by a short sharp noise as they pass within an inch of the ear, the head, or the breast.

To add to all this, compassion strikes the beating heart with pity at the sight of the maimed and fallen. The young soldier cannot reach any of these different strata of danger without feeling that the light of reason does not move here in the same medium, that it is not refracted in the same manner as in speculative contemplation. Indeed, he must be a very extraordinary man who, under these impressions for the first time, does not lose the power of making any instantaneous decisions. It is true that habit soon blunts such impressions; in half in hour we begin to be more or less indifferent to all that is going on around us: but an ordinary character never attains to complete coolness and the natural elasticity of mind; and so we perceive that here again ordinary qualities will not suffice—a thing which gains truth, the wider the sphere of activity which is to be filled. Enthusiastic, stoical, natural bravery, great ambition, or also long familiarity with danger—much of all this there must be if all the effects produced in this resistant medium are not to fall far short of that which in the student's chamber may appear only the ordinary standard.

Danger in War belongs to its friction; a correct idea of its influence is necessary for truth of perception, and therefore it is brought under notice here.

CHAPTER V. Of Bodily Exertion in War

If no one were allowed to pass an opinion on the events of War, except at a moment when he is benumbed by frost, sinking from heat and thirst, or dying with hunger and fatigue, we should certainly have fewer judgments correct objectively; but they would be so, subjectively, at least; that is, they would contain in themselves the exact relation between the person giving the judgment and the object. We can perceive this by observing how modestly subdued, even spiritless and desponding, is the opinion passed upon the results of untoward events by those who have been eye-witnesses, but especially if they have been parties concerned. This is, according to our view, a criterion of the influence which bodily fatigue exercises, and of the allowance to be made for it in matters of opinion.

Amongst the many things in War for which no tariff can be fixed, bodily effort may be specially reckoned. Provided there is no waste, it is a coefficient of all the forces, and no one can tell exactly to what extent it may be carried. But what is remarkable is, that just as only a strong arm enables the archer to stretch the bowstring to the utmost extent, so also in War it is only by means of a great directing spirit that we can expect the full power latent in the troops to be developed. For it is one thing if an Army, in consequence of great misfortunes, surrounded with danger, falls all to pieces like a wall that has been thrown down, and can only find safety in the utmost exertion of its bodily strength; it is another thing entirely when a victorious Army, drawn on by proud feelings only, is conducted at the will of its Chief. The same effort which in the one case might at most excite our pity must in the other call forth our admiration, because it is much more difficult to sustain.

By this comes to light for the inexperienced eye one of those things which put fetters in the dark, as it were, on the action of the mind, and wear out in secret the powers of the soul.

Although here the question is strictly only respecting the extreme effort required by a Commander from his Army, by a leader from his followers, therefore of the spirit to demand it and of the art of getting it, still the personal physical exertion of Generals and of the Chief Commander must not be overlooked. Having brought the analysis of War conscientiously up to this point, we could not but take account also of the weight of this small remaining residue.

We have spoken here of bodily effort, chiefly because, like danger, it belongs to the fundamental causes of friction, and because its indefinite quantity makes it like an elastic body, the friction of which is well known to be difficult to calculate.

To check the abuse of these considerations, of such a survey of things which aggravate the difficulties of War, nature has given our judgment a guide in our sensibilities, just as an individual cannot with advantage refer to his personal deficiencies if he is insulted and ill-treated, but may well do so if he has successfully repelled the affront, or has fully revenged it, so no Commander or Army will lessen the impression of a disgraceful defeat by depicting the danger, the distress, the exertions, things which would immensely enhance the glory of a victory. Thus our feeling, which after all is only a higher kind of judgment, forbids us to do what seems an act of justice to which our judgment would be inclined.

CHAPTER VI. Information in War

By the word "information" we denote all the knowledge which we have of the enemy and his country; therefore, in fact, the foundation of all our ideas and actions. Let us just consider the nature of this foundation, its want of trustworthiness, its changefulness, and we shall soon feel what a dangerous edifice War is, how easily it may fall to pieces and bury us in its ruins. For although it is a maxim in all books that we should trust only certain information, that we must be always suspicious, that is only a miserable book comfort, belonging to that description of knowledge in which writers of systems and compendiums take refuge for want of anything better to say.

Great part of the information obtained in War is contradictory, a still greater part is false, and by far the greatest part is of a doubtful character. What is required of an officer is a certain power of discrimination, which only knowledge of men and things and good judgment can give. The law of probability must be his guide. This is not a trifling difficulty even in respect of the first plans, which can be formed in the chamber outside the real sphere of War, but it is enormously increased when in the thick of War itself one report follows hard upon the heels of another; it is then fortunate if these reports in contradicting each other show a certain balance of probability, and thus themselves call forth a scrutiny. It is much worse for the inexperienced when accident does not render him this service, but one report supports another, confirms it, magnifies it, finishes off the picture with fresh touches of colour, until necessity in urgent haste forces from us a resolution which will soon be discovered to be folly, all those reports having been lies, exaggerations, errors, &c. &c. In a few words, most reports are false, and the timidity of men acts as a multiplier of lies and untruths. As a general rule, every one is more inclined to lend credence to the bad than the good. Every one is inclined to magnify the bad in some measure, and although the alarms which are thus propagated like the waves of the sea subside into themselves, still, like them, without any apparent cause they rise again. Firm in reliance on his own better convictions, the Chief must stand like a rock against which the sea breaks its fury in vain. The rôle is not easy; he who is not by nature of a buoyant disposition, or trained by experience in War, and matured in judgment, may let it be his rule to do violence to his own natural conviction by inclining from the side of fear to that of hope; only by that means will he be able to preserve his balance. This difficulty of seeing things correctly, which is one of the greatest sources of friction in War, makes things appear quite different from what was expected. The impression of the senses is stronger than the force of the ideas resulting from methodical reflection, and this goes so far that no important undertaking was ever yet carried out without the Commander having to subdue new doubts in himself at the time of commencing the execution of his work. Ordinary men who follow the suggestions of others become, therefore, generally undecided on the spot; they think that they have found circumstances different from what they had expected, and this view gains strength by their again yielding to the suggestions of others. But even the man who has made his own plans, when he comes to see things with his own eyes will often think he has done wrong. Firm reliance on self must make him proof against the seeming pressure of the moment; his first conviction will in the end prove true, when the foreground scenery which fate has pushed on to the stage of War, with its accompaniments of terrific objects, is drawn aside and the horizon extended. This is one of the great chasms which separate conception from execution.

CHAPTER VII. Friction in War

As long as we have no personal knowledge of War, we cannot conceive where those difficulties lie of which so much is said, and what that genius and those extraordinary mental powers required in a General have really to do. All appears so simple, all the requisite branches of knowledge appear so plain, all the combinations so unimportant, that in comparison with them the easiest problem in higher mathematics impresses us with a certain scientific dignity. But if we have seen War, all becomes intelligible; and still, after all, it is extremely difficult to describe what it is which brings about this change, to specify this invisible and completely efficient factor.

Everything is very simple in War, but the simplest thing is difficult. These difficulties accumulate and produce a friction which no man can imagine exactly who has not seen War, Suppose now a traveller, who towards evening expects to accomplish the two stages at the end of his day's journey, four or five leagues, with post-horses, on the high road—it is nothing. He arrives now at the last station but one, finds no horses, or very bad ones; then a hilly country, bad roads; it is a dark night, and he is glad when, after a great deal of trouble, he reaches the next station, and finds there some miserable accommodation. So in War, through the influence of an infinity of petty circumstances, which cannot properly be described on paper, things disappoint us, and we fall short of the mark. A powerful iron will overcomes this friction; it crushes the obstacles, but certainly the machine along with them. We shall often meet with this result. Like an obelisk towards which the principal streets of a town converge, the strong will of a proud spirit stands prominent and commanding in the middle of the Art of War.

Friction is the only conception which in a general way corresponds to that which distinguishes real War from War on paper. The military machine, the Army and all belonging to it, is in fact simple, and appears on this account easy to manage. But let us reflect that no part of it is in one piece, that it is composed entirely of individuals, each of which keeps up its own friction in all directions. Theoretically all sounds very well: the commander of a battalion is responsible for the execution of the order given; and as the battalion by its discipline is glued together into one piece, and the chief must be a man of acknowledged zeal, the beam turns on an iron pin with little friction. But it is not so in reality, and all that is exaggerated and false in such a conception manifests itself at once in War. The battalion always remains composed of a number of men, of whom, if chance so wills, the most insignificant is able to occasion delay and even irregularity. The danger which War brings with it, the bodily exertions which it requires, augment this evil so much that they may be regarded as the greatest causes of it.

This enormous friction, which is not concentrated, as in mechanics, at a few points, is therefore everywhere brought into contact with chance, and thus incidents take place upon which it was impossible to calculate, their chief origin being chance. As an instance of one such chance: the weather. Here the fog prevents the enemy from being discovered in time, a battery from firing at the right moment, a report from reaching the General; there the rain prevents a battalion from arriving at the right time, because instead of for three it had to march perhaps eight hours; the cavalry from charging effectively because it is stuck fast in heavy ground.

These are only a few incidents of detail by way of elucidation, that the reader may be able to follow the author, for whole volumes might be written on these difficulties. To avoid this, and still to give a clear conception of the host of small difficulties to be contended with in War, we might go on heaping up illustrations, if we were not afraid of being tiresome. But those who have already comprehended us will permit us to add a few more.

Activity in War is movement in a resistant medium. Just as a man immersed in water is unable to perform with ease and regularity the most natural and simplest movement, that of walking, so in War, with ordinary powers, one cannot keep even the line of mediocrity. This is the reason that the correct theorist is like a swimming master, who teaches on dry land movements which are required in the water, which must appear grotesque and ludicrous to those who forget about the water. This is also why theorists, who have never plunged in themselves, or who cannot deduce any generalities from their experience, are unpractical and even absurd, because they only teach what every one knows—how to walk.

Further, every War is rich in particular facts, while at the same time each is an unexplored sea, full of rocks which the General may have a suspicion of, but which he has never seen with his eye, and round which, moreover, he must steer in the night. If a contrary wind also springs up, that is, if any great accidental event declares itself adverse to him, then the most consummate skill, presence of mind, and energy are required, whilst to those who only look on from a distance all seems to proceed with the utmost ease. The knowledge of this friction is a chief part of that so often talked of, experience in War, which is required in a good General. Certainly he is not the best General in whose mind it assumes the greatest dimensions, who is the most over-awed by it (this includes that class of over-anxious Generals, of whom there are so many amongst the experienced); but a General must be aware of it that he may overcome it, where that is possible, and that he may not expect a degree of precision in results which is impossible on account of this very friction. Besides, it can never be learnt theoretically; and if it could, there would still be wanting that experience of judgment which is called tact, and which is always more necessary in a field full of innumerable small and diversified objects than in great and decisive cases, when one's own judgment may be aided by consultation with others. Just as the man of the world, through tact of judgment which has become habit, speaks, acts, and moves only as suits the occasion, so the officer experienced in War will always, in great and small matters, at every pulsation of War as we may say, decide and determine suitably to the occasion. Through this experience and practice the idea comes to his mind of itself that so and so will not suit. And thus he will not easily place himself in a position by which he is compromised, which, if it often occurs in War, shakes all the foundations of confidence and becomes extremely dangerous.

It is therefore this friction, or what is so termed here, which makes that which appears easy in War difficult in reality. As we proceed, we shall often meet with this subject again, and it will hereafter become plain that besides experience and a strong will, there are still many other rare qualities of the mind required to make a man a consummate General.

CHAPTER VIII. Concluding Remarks, Book I

Those things which as elements meet together in the atmosphere of War and make it a resistant medium for every activity we have designated under the terms danger, bodily effort (exertion), information, and friction. In their impedient effects they may therefore be comprehended again in the collective notion of a general friction. Now is there, then, no kind of oil which is capable of diminishing this friction? Only one, and that one is not always available at the will of the Commander or his Army. It is the habituation of an Army to War.

Habit gives strength to the body in great exertion, to the mind in great danger, to the judgment against first impressions. By it a valuable circumspection is generally gained throughout every rank, from the hussar and rifleman up to the General of Division, which facilitates the work of the Chief Commander.

As the human eye in a dark room dilates its pupil, draws in the little light that there is, partially distinguishes objects by degrees, and at last knows them quite well, so it is in War with the experienced soldier, whilst the novice is only met by pitch dark night.

Habituation to War no General can give his Army at once, and the camps of manœuvre (peace exercises) furnish but a weak substitute for it, weak in comparison with real experience in War, but not weak in relation to other Armies in which the training is limited to mere mechanical exercises of routine. So to regulate the exercises in peace time as to include some of these causes of friction, that the judgment, circumspection, even resolution of the separate leaders may be brought into exercise, is of much greater consequence than those believe who do not know the thing by experience. It is of immense importance that the soldier, high or low, whatever rank he has, should not have to encounter in War those things which, when seen for the first time, set him in astonishment and perplexity; if he has only met with them one single time before, even by that he is half acquainted with them. This relates even to bodily fatigues. They should be practised less to accustom the body to them than the mind. In War the young soldier is very apt to regard unusual fatigues as the consequence of faults, mistakes, and embarrassment in the conduct of the whole, and to become distressed and despondent as a consequence. This would not happen if he had been prepared for this beforehand by exercises in peace.

Another less comprehensive but still very important means of gaining habituation to War in time of peace is to invite into the service officers of foreign armies who have had experience in War. Peace seldom reigns over all Europe, and never in all quarters of the world. A State which has been long at peace should, therefore, always seek to procure some officers who have done good service at the different scenes of Warfare, or to send there some of its own, that they may get a lesson in War.

However small the number of officers of this description may appear in proportion to the mass, still their influence is very sensibly felt.(*) Their experience, the bent of their genius, the stamp of their character, influence their subordinates and comrades; and besides that, if they cannot be placed in positions of superior command, they may always be regarded as men acquainted with the country, who may be questioned on many special occasions.

END OF BOOK ONE

BOOK II: ON THE THEORY OF WAR

CHAPTER I. Branches of the Art of War

War in its literal meaning is fighting, for fighting alone is the efficient principle in the manifold activity which in a wide sense is called War. But fighting is a trial of strength of the moral and physical forces by means of the latter. That the moral cannot be omitted is evident of itself, for the condition of the mind has always the most decisive influence on the forces employed in War.

The necessity of fighting very soon led men to special inventions to turn the advantage in it in their own favour: in consequence of these the mode of fighting has undergone great alterations; but in whatever way it is conducted its conception remains unaltered, and fighting is that which constitutes War.

The inventions have been from the first weapons and equipments for the individual combatants. These have to be provided and the use of them learnt before the War begins. They are made suitable to the nature of the fighting, consequently are ruled by it; but plainly the activity engaged in these appliances is a different thing from the fight itself; it is only the preparation for the combat, not the conduct of the same. That arming and equipping are not essential to the conception of fighting is plain, because mere wrestling is also fighting.

Fighting has determined everything appertaining to arms and equipment, and these in turn modify the mode of fighting; there is, therefore, a reciprocity of action between the two.

Nevertheless, the fight itself remains still an entirely special activity, more particularly because it moves in an entirely special element, namely, in the element of danger.

If, then, there is anywhere a necessity for drawing a line between two different activities, it is here; and in order to see clearly the importance of this idea, we need only just to call to mind how often eminent personal fitness in one field has turned out nothing but the most useless pedantry in the other.

It is also in no way difficult to separate in idea the one activity from the other, if we look at the combatant forces fully armed and equipped as a given means, the profitable use of which requires nothing more than a knowledge of their general results.

The Art of War is therefore, in its proper sense, the art of making use of the given means in fighting, and we cannot give it a better name than the "Conduct of War." On the other hand, in a wider sense all activities which have their existence on account of War, therefore the whole creation of troops, that is levying them, arming, equipping, and exercising them, belong to the Art of War.

To make a sound theory it is most essential to separate these two activities, for it is easy to see that if every act of War is to begin with the preparation of military forces, and to presuppose forces so organised as a primary condition for conducting War, that theory will only be applicable in the few cases to which the force available happens to be exactly suited. If, on the other hand, we wish to have a theory which shall suit most cases, and will not be wholly useless in any case, it must be founded on those means which are in most general use, and in respect to these only on the actual results springing from them.

The conduct of War is, therefore, the formation and conduct of the fighting. If this fighting was a single act, there would be no necessity for any further subdivision, but the fight is composed of a greater or less number of single acts, complete in themselves, which we call combats, as we have shown in the first chapter of the first book, and which form new units. From this arises the totally different activities, that of the formation and conduct of these single combats in themselves, and the combination of them with one another, with a view to the ultimate object of the War. The first is called tactics, the other strategy.

This division into tactics and strategy is now in almost general use, and every one knows tolerably well under which head to place any single fact, without knowing very distinctly the grounds on which the classification is founded. But when such divisions are blindly adhered to in practice, they must have some deep root. We have searched for this root, and we might say that it is just the usage of the majority which has brought us to it. On the other hand, we look upon the arbitrary, unnatural definitions of these conceptions sought to be established by some writers as not in accordance with the general usage of the terms.

According to our classification, therefore, tactics is the theory of the use of military forces in combat. Strategy is the theory of the use of combats for the object of the War.

The way in which the conception of a single, or independent combat, is more closely determined, the conditions to which this unit is attached, we shall only be able to explain clearly when we consider the combat; we must content ourselves for the present with saying that in relation to space, therefore in combats taking place at the same time, the unit reaches just as far as personal command reaches; but in regard to time, and therefore in relation to combats which follow each other in close succession, it reaches to the moment when the crisis which takes place in every combat is entirely passed.

That doubtful cases may occur, cases, for instance, in which several combats may perhaps be regarded also as a single one, will not overthrow the ground of distinction we have adopted, for the same is the case with all grounds of distinction of real things which are differentiated by a gradually diminishing scale. There may, therefore, certainly be acts of activity in War which, without any alteration in the point of view, may just as well be counted strategic as tactical; for example, very extended positions resembling a chain of posts, the preparations for the passage of a river at several points, &c.

Our classification reaches and covers only the use of the military force. But now there are in War a number of activities which are subservient to it, and still are quite different from it; sometimes closely allied, sometimes less near in their affinity. All these activities relate to the maintenance of the military force. In the same way as its creation and training precede its use, so its maintenance is always a necessary condition. But, strictly viewed, all activities thus connected with it are always to be regarded only as preparations for fighting; they are certainly nothing more than activities which are very close to the action, so that they run through the hostile act alternate in importance with the use of the forces. We have therefore a right to exclude them as well as the other preparatory activities from the Art of War in its restricted sense, from the conduct of War properly so called; and we are obliged to do so if we would comply with the first principle of all theory, the elimination of all heterogeneous elements. Who would include in the real "conduct of War" the whole litany of subsistence and administration, because it is admitted to stand in constant reciprocal action with the use of the troops, but is something essentially different from it?

We have said, in the third chapter of our first book, that as the fight or combat is the only directly effective activity, therefore the threads of all others, as they end in it, are included in it. By this we meant to say that to all others an object was thereby appointed which, in accordance with the laws peculiar to themselves, they must seek to attain. Here we must go a little closer into this subject.

The subjects which constitute the activities outside of the combat are of various kinds.

The one part belongs, in one respect, to the combat itself, is identical with it, whilst it serves in another respect for the maintenance of the military force. The other part belongs purely to the subsistence, and has only, in consequence of the reciprocal action, a limited influence on the combats by its results. The subjects which in one respect belong to the fighting itself are marches, camps, and cantonments, for they suppose so many different situations of troops, and where troops are supposed there the idea of the combat must always be present.

The other subjects, which only belong to the maintenance, are subsistence, care of the sick, the supply and repair of arms and equipment.

Marches are quite identical with the use of the troops. The act of marching in the combat, generally called manoeuvring, certainly does not necessarily include the use of weapons, but it is so completely and necessarily combined with it that it forms an integral part of that which we call a combat. But the march outside the combat is nothing but the execution of a strategic measure. By the strategic plan is settled when, where, and with what forces a battle is to be delivered—and to carry that into execution the march is the only means.

The march outside of the combat is therefore an instrument of strategy, but not on that account exclusively a subject of strategy, for as the armed force which executes it may be involved in a possible combat at any moment, therefore its execution stands also under tactical as well as strategic rules. If we prescribe to a column its route on a particular side of a river or of a branch of a mountain, then that is a strategic measure, for it contains the intention of fighting on that particular side of the hill or river in preference to the other, in case a combat should be necessary during the march.

But if a column, instead of following the road through a valley, marches along the parallel ridge of heights, or for the convenience of marching divides itself into several columns, then these are tactical arrangements, for they relate to the manner in which we shall use the troops in the anticipated combat.

The particular order of march is in constant relation with readiness for combat, is therefore tactical in its nature, for it is nothing more than the first or preliminary disposition for the battle which may possibly take place.

As the march is the instrument by which strategy apportions its active elements, the combats, but these last often only appear by their results and not in the details of their real course, it could not fail to happen that in theory the instrument has often been substituted for the efficient principle. Thus we hear of a decisive skilful march, allusion being thereby made to those combat-combinations to which these marches led. This substitution of ideas is too natural and conciseness of expression too desirable to call for alteration, but still it is only a condensed chain of ideas in regard to which we must never omit to bear in mind the full meaning, if we would avoid falling into error.

We fall into an error of this description if we attribute to strategical combinations a power independent of tactical results. We read of marches and manœuvres combined, the object attained, and at the same time not a word about combat, from which the conclusion is drawn that there are means in War of conquering an enemy without fighting. The prolific nature of this error we cannot show until hereafter.

But although a march can be regarded absolutely as an integral part of the combat, still there are in it certain relations which do not belong to the combat, and therefore are neither tactical nor strategic. To these belong all arrangements which concern only the accommodation of the troops, the construction of bridges, roads, &c. These are only conditions; under many circumstances they are in very close connection, and may almost identify themselves with the troops, as in building a bridge in presence of the enemy; but in themselves they are always activities, the theory of which does not form part of the theory of the conduct of War.

Camps, by which we mean every disposition of troops in concentrated, therefore in battle order, in contradistinction to cantonments or quarters, are a state of rest, therefore of restoration; but they are at the same time also the strategic appointment of a battle on the spot, chosen; and by the manner in which they are taken up they contain the fundamental lines of the battle, a condition from which every defensive battle starts; they are therefore essential parts of both strategy and tactics.

Cantonments take the place of camps for the better refreshment of the troops. They are therefore, like camps, strategic subjects as regards position and extent; tactical subjects as regards internal organisation, with a view to readiness to fight.

The occupation of camps and cantonments no doubt usually combines with the recuperation of the troops another object also, for example, the covering a district of country, the holding a position; but it can very well be only the first. We remind our readers that strategy may follow a great diversity of objects, for everything which appears an advantage may be the object of a combat, and the preservation of the instrument with which War is made must necessarily very often become the object of its partial combinations.

If, therefore, in such a case strategy ministers only to the maintenance of the troops, we are not on that account out of the field of strategy, for we are still engaged with the use of the military force, because every disposition of that force upon any point Whatever of the theatre of War is such a use.

But if the maintenance of the troops in camp or quarters calls forth activities which are no employment of the armed force, such as the construction of huts, pitching of tents, subsistence and sanitary services in camps or quarters, then such belong neither to strategy nor tactics.

Even entrenchments, the site and preparation of which are plainly part of the order of battle, therefore tactical subjects, do not belong to the theory of the conduct of War so far as respects the execution of their construction the knowledge and skill required for such work being, in point of fact, qualities inherent in the nature of an organised Army; the theory of the combat takes them for granted.

Amongst the subjects which belong to the mere keeping up of an armed force, because none of the parts are identified with the combat, the victualling of the troops themselves comes first, as it must be done almost daily and for each individual. Thus it is that it completely permeates military action in the parts constituting strategy—we say parts constituting strategy, because during a battle the subsistence of troops will rarely have any influence in modifying the plan, although the thing is conceivable enough. The care for the subsistence of the troops comes therefore into reciprocal action chiefly with strategy, and there is nothing more common than for the leading strategic features of a campaign and War to be traced out in connection with a view to this supply. But however frequent and however important these views of supply may be, the subsistence of the troops always remains a completely different activity from the use of the troops, and the former has only an influence on the latter by its results.

The other branches of administrative activity which we have mentioned stand much farther apart from the use of the troops. The care of sick and wounded, highly important as it is for the good of an Army, directly affects it only in a small portion of the individuals composing it, and therefore has only a weak and indirect influence upon the use of the rest. The completing and replacing articles of arms and equipment, except so far as by the organism of the forces it constitutes a continuous activity inherent in them—takes place only periodically, and therefore seldom affects strategic plans.

We must, however, here guard ourselves against a mistake. In certain cases these subjects may be really of decisive importance. The distance of hospitals and depôts of munitions may very easily be imagined as the sole cause of very important strategic decisions. We do not wish either to contest that point or to throw it into the shade. But we are at present occupied not with the particular facts of a concrete case, but with abstract theory; and our assertion therefore is that such an influence is too rare to give the theory of sanitary measures and the supply of munitions and arms an importance in theory of the conduct of War such as to make it worthwhile to include in the theory of the conduct of War the consideration of the different ways and systems which the above theories may furnish, in the same way as is certainly necessary in regard to victualling troops.

If we have clearly understood the results of our reflections, then the activities belonging to War divide themselves into two principal classes, into such as are only "preparations for War" and into the "War itself." This division must therefore also be made in theory.

The knowledge and applications of skill in the preparations for War are engaged in the creation, discipline, and maintenance of all the military forces; what general names should be given to them we do not enter into, but we see that artillery, fortification, elementary tactics, as they are called, the whole organisation and administration of the various armed forces, and all such things are included. But the theory of War itself occupies itself with the use of these prepared means for the object of the war. It needs of the first only the results, that is, the knowledge of the principal properties of the means taken in hand for use. This we call "The Art of War" in a limited sense, or "Theory of the Conduct of War," or "Theory of the Employment of Armed Forces," all of them denoting for us the same thing.

The present theory will therefore treat the combat as the real contest, marches, camps, and cantonments as circumstances which are more or less identical with it. The subsistence of the troops will only come into consideration like other given circumstances in respect of its results, not as an activity belonging to the combat.

The Art of War thus viewed in its limited sense divides itself again into tactics and strategy. The former occupies itself with the form of the separate combat, the latter with its use. Both connect themselves with the circumstances of marches, camps, cantonments only through the combat, and these circumstances are tactical or strategic according as they relate to the form or to the signification of the battle.

No doubt there will be many readers who will consider superfluous this careful separation of two things lying so close together as tactics and strategy, because it has no direct effect on the conduct itself of War. We admit, certainly that it would be pedantry to look for direct effects on the field of battle from a theoretical distinction.

But the first business of every theory is to clear up conceptions and ideas which have been jumbled together, and, we may say, entangled and confused; and only when a right understanding is established, as to names and conceptions, can we hope to progress with clearness and facility, and be certain that author and reader will always see things from the same point of view. Tactics and strategy are two activities mutually permeating each other in time and space, at the same time essentially different activities, the inner laws and mutual relations of which cannot be intelligible at all to the mind until a clear conception of the nature of each activity is established.

He to whom all this is nothing, must either repudiate all theoretical consideration, or his understanding has not as yet been pained by the confused and perplexing ideas resting on no fixed point of view, leading to no satisfactory result, sometimes dull, sometimes fantastic, sometimes floating in vague generalities, which we are often obliged to hear and read on the conduct of War, owing to the spirit of scientific investigation having hitherto been little directed to these subjects.

CHAPTER II. On the Theory of War

1. THE FIRST CONCEPTION OF THE "ART OF WAR" WAS MERELY THE PREPARATION OF THE ARMED FORCES.

Formerly by the term "Art of War," or "Science of War," nothing was understood but the totality of those branches of knowledge and those appliances of skill occupied with material things. The pattern and preparation and the mode of using arms, the construction of fortifications and entrenchments, the organism of an army and the mechanism of its movements, were the subject; these branches of knowledge and skill above referred to, and the end and aim of them all was the establishment of an armed force fit for use in War. All this concerned merely things belonging to the material world and a one-sided activity only, and it was in fact nothing but an activity advancing by gradations from the lower occupations to a finer kind of mechanical art. The relation of all this to War itself was very much the same as the relation of the art of the sword cutler to the art of using the sword. The employment in the moment of danger and in a state of constant reciprocal action of the particular energies of mind and spirit in the direction proposed to them was not yet even mooted.

2. TRUE WAR FIRST APPEARS IN THE ART OF SIEGES.

In the art of sieges we first perceive a certain degree of guidance of the combat, something of the action of the intellectual faculties upon the material forces placed under their control, but generally only so far that it very soon embodied itself again in new material forms, such as approaches, trenches, counter-approaches, batteries, &c., and every step which this action of the higher faculties took was marked by some such result; it was only the thread that was required on which to string these material inventions in order. As the intellect can hardly manifest itself in this kind of War, except in such things, so therefore nearly all that was necessary was done in that way.

3. THEN TACTICS TRIED TO FIND ITS WAY IN THE SAME DIRECTION.

Afterwards tactics attempted to give to the mechanism of its joints the character of a general disposition, built upon the peculiar properties of the instrument, which character leads indeed to the battle-field, but instead of leading to the free activity of mind, leads to an Army made like an automaton by its rigid formations and orders of battle, which, movable only by the word of command, is intended to unwind its activities like a piece of clockwork.

4. THE REAL CONDUCT OF WAR ONLY MADE ITS APPEARANCE INCIDENTALLY AND INCOGNITO.

The conduct of War properly so called, that is, a use of the prepared means adapted to the most special requirements, was not considered as any suitable subject for theory, but one which should be left to natural talents alone. By degrees, as War passed from the hand-to-hand encounters of the middle ages into a more regular and systematic form, stray reflections on this point also forced themselves into men's minds, but they mostly appeared only incidentally in memoirs and narratives, and in a certain measure incognito.

5. REFLECTIONS ON MILITARY EVENTS BROUGHT ABOUT THE WANT OF A THEORY.

As contemplation on War continually increased, and its history every day assumed more of a critical character, the urgent want appeared of the support of fixed maxims and rules, in order that in the controversies naturally arising about military events the war of opinions might be brought to some one point. This whirl of opinions, which neither revolved on any central pivot nor according to any appreciable laws, could not but be very distasteful to people's minds.

6. ENDEAVOURS TO ESTABLISH A POSITIVE THEORY.

There arose, therefore, an endeavour to establish maxims, rules, and even systems for the conduct of War. By this the attainment of a positive object was proposed, without taking into view the endless difficulties which the conduct of War presents in that respect. The conduct of War, as we have shown, has no definite limits in any direction, while every system has the circumscribing nature of a synthesis, from which results an irreconcileable opposition between such a theory and practice.

7. LIMITATION TO MATERIAL OBJECTS.

Writers on theory felt the difficulty of the subject soon enough, and thought themselves entitled to get rid of it by directing their maxims and systems only upon material things and a one-sided activity. Their aim was to reach results, as in the science for the preparation for War, entirely certain and positive, and therefore only to take into consideration that which could be made matter of calculation.

8. SUPERIORITY OF NUMBERS.

The superiority in numbers being a material condition, it was chosen from amongst all the factors required to produce victory, because it could be brought under mathematical laws through combinations of time and space. It was thought possible to leave out of sight all other circumstances, by supposing them to be equal on each side, and therefore to neutralise one another. This would have been very well if it had been done to gain a preliminary knowledge of this one factor, according to its relations, but to make it a rule for ever to consider superiority of numbers as the sole law; to see the whole secret of the Art of War in the formula, in a certain time, at a certain point, to bring up superior masses—was a restriction overruled by the force of realities.

9. VICTUALLING OF TROOPS.

By one theoretical school an attempt was made to systematise another material element also, by making the subsistence of troops, according to a previously established organism of the Army, the supreme legislator in the higher conduct of War. In this way certainly they arrived at definite figures, but at figures which rested on a number of arbitrary calculations, and which therefore could not stand the test of practical application.

10. BASE.

An ingenious author tried to concentrate in a single conception, that of a BASE, a whole host of objects amongst which sundry relations even with immaterial forces found their way in as well. The list comprised the subsistence of the troops, the keeping them complete in numbers and equipment, the security of communications with the home country, lastly, the security of retreat in case it became necessary; and, first of all, he proposed to substitute this conception of a base for all these things; then for the base itself to substitute its own length (extent); and, last of all, to substitute the angle formed by the army with this base: all this was done to obtain a pure geometrical result utterly useless. This last is, in fact, unavoidable, if we reflect that none of these substitutions could be made without violating truth and leaving out some of the things contained in the original conception. The idea of a base is a real necessity for strategy, and to have conceived it is meritorious; but to make such a use of it as we have depicted is completely inadmissible, and could not but lead to partial conclusions which have forced these theorists into a direction opposed to common sense, namely, to a belief in the decisive effect of the enveloping form of attack.

11. INTERIOR LINES.

As a reaction against this false direction, another geometrical principle, that of the so-called interior lines, was then elevated to the throne. Although this principle rests on a sound foundation, on the truth that the combat is the only effectual means in War, still it is, just on account of its purely geometrical nature, nothing but another case of one-sided theory which can never gain ascendency in the real world.

12. ALL THESE ATTEMPTS ARE OPEN TO OBJECTION.

All these attempts at theory are only to be considered in their analytical part as progress in the province of truth, but in their synthetical part, in their precepts and rules, they are quite unserviceable.

They strive after determinate quantities, whilst in War all is undetermined, and the calculation has always to be made with varying quantities.

They direct the attention only upon material forces, while the whole military action is penetrated throughout by intelligent forces and their effects.

They only pay regard to activity on one side, whilst War is a constant state of reciprocal action, the effects of which are mutual.

13. AS A RULE THEY EXCLUDE GENIUS.

All that was not attainable by such miserable philosophy, the offspring of partial views, lay outside the precincts of science—and was the field of genius, which RAISES ITSELF ABOVE RULES.

Pity the warrior who is contented to crawl about in this beggardom of rules, which are too bad for genius, over which it can set itself superior, over which it can perchance make merry! What genius does must be the best of all rules, and theory cannot do better than to show how and why it is so.

Pity the theory which sets itself in opposition to the mind! It cannot repair this contradiction by any humility, and the humbler it is so much the sooner will ridicule and contempt drive it out of real life.

14. THE DIFFICULTY OF THEORY AS SOON AS MORAL QUANTITIES COME INTO CONSIDERATION.

Every theory becomes infinitely more difficult from the moment that it touches on the province of moral quantities. Architecture and painting know quite well what they are about as long as they have only to do with matter; there is no dispute about mechanical or optical construction. But as soon as the moral activities begin their work, as soon as moral impressions and feelings are produced, the whole set of rules dissolves into vague ideas.

The science of medicine is chiefly engaged with bodily phenomena only; its business is with the animal organism, which, liable to perpetual change, is never exactly the same for two moments. This makes its practice very difficult, and places the judgment of the physician above his science; but how much more difficult is the case if a moral effect is added, and how much higher must we place the physician of the mind?

15. THE MORAL QUANTITIES MUST NOT BE EXCLUDED IN WAR.

But now the activity in War is never directed solely against matter; it is always at the same time directed against the intelligent force which gives life to this matter, and to separate the two from each other is impossible.

But the intelligent forces are only visible to the inner eye, and this is different in each person, and often different in the same person at different times.

As danger is the general element in which everything moves in War, it is also chiefly by courage, the feeling of one's own power, that the judgment is differently influenced. It is to a certain extent the crystalline lens through which all appearances pass before reaching the understanding.

And yet we cannot doubt that these things acquire a certain objective value simply through experience.

Every one knows the moral effect of a surprise, of an attack in flank or rear. Every one thinks less of the enemy's courage as soon as he turns his back, and ventures much more in pursuit than when pursued. Every one judges of the enemy's General by his reputed talents, by his age and experience, and shapes his course accordingly. Every one casts a scrutinising glance at the spirit and feeling of his own and the enemy's troops. All these and similar effects in the province of the moral nature of man have established themselves by experience, are perpetually recurring, and therefore warrant our reckoning them as real quantities of their kind. What could we do with any theory which should leave them out of consideration?

Certainly experience is an indispensable title for these truths. With psychological and philosophical sophistries no theory, no General, should meddle.

16. PRINCIPAL DIFFICULTY OF A THEORY FOR THE CONDUCT OF WAR.

In order to comprehend clearly the difficulty of the proposition which is contained in a theory for the conduct of War, and thence to deduce the necessary characteristics of such a theory, we must take a closer view of the chief particulars which make up the nature of activity in War.

17. FIRST SPECIALITY.—MORAL FORCES AND THEIR EFFECTS. (HOSTILE FEELING.)

The first of these specialities consists in the moral forces and effects.

The combat is, in its origin, the expression of hostile feeling, but in our great combats, which we call Wars, the hostile feeling frequently resolves itself into merely a hostile view, and there is usually no innate hostile feeling residing in individual against individual. Nevertheless, the combat never passes off without such feelings being brought into activity. National hatred, which is seldom wanting in our Wars, is a substitute for personal hostility in the breast of individual opposed to individual. But where this also is wanting, and at first no animosity of feeling subsists, a hostile feeling is kindled by the combat itself; for an act of violence which any one commits upon us by order of his superior, will excite in us a desire to retaliate and be revenged on him, sooner than on the superior power at whose command the act was done. This is human, or animal if we will; still it is so. We are very apt to regard the combat in theory as an abstract trial of strength, without any participation on the part of the feelings, and that is one of the thousand errors which theorists deliberately commit, because they do not see its consequences.

Besides that excitation of feelings naturally arising from the combat itself, there are others also which do not essentially belong to it, but which, on account of their relationship, easily unite with it—ambition, love of power, enthusiasm of every kind, &c. &c.

18. THE IMPRESSIONS OF DANGER. (COURAGE.)

Finally, the combat begets the element of danger, in which all the activities of War must live and move, like the bird in the air or the fish in the water. But the influences of danger all pass into the feelings, either directly—that is, instinctively—or through the medium of the understanding. The effect in the first case would be a desire to escape from the danger, and, if that cannot be done, fright and anxiety. If this effect does not take place, then it is courage, which is a counterpoise to that instinct. Courage is, however, by no means an act of the understanding, but likewise a feeling, like fear; the latter looks to the physical preservation, courage to the moral preservation. Courage, then, is a nobler instinct. But because it is so, it will not allow itself to be used as a lifeless instrument, which produces its effects exactly according to prescribed measure. Courage is therefore no mere counterpoise to danger in order to neutralise the latter in its effects, but a peculiar power in itself.

19. EXTENT OF THE INFLUENCE OF DANGER.

But to estimate exactly the influence of danger upon the principal actors in War, we must not limit its sphere to the physical danger of the moment. It dominates over the actor, not only by threatening him, but also by threatening all entrusted to him, not only at the moment in which it is actually present, but also through the imagination at all other moments, which have a connection with the present; lastly, not only directly by itself, but also indirectly by the responsibility which makes it bear with tenfold weight on the mind of the chief actor. Who could advise, or resolve upon a great battle, without feeling his mind more or less wrought up, or perplexed by, the danger and responsibility which such a great act of decision carries in itself? We may say that action in War, in so far as it is real action, not a mere condition, is never out of the sphere of danger.

20. OTHER POWERS OF FEELING.

If we look upon these affections which are excited by hostility and danger as peculiarly belonging to War, we do not, therefore, exclude from it all others accompanying man in his life's journey.

They will also find room here frequently enough. Certainly we may say that many a petty action of the passions is silenced in this serious business of life; but that holds good only in respect to those acting in a lower sphere, who, hurried on from one state of danger and exertion to another, lose sight of the rest of the things of life, become unused to deceit, because it is of no avail with death, and so attain to that soldierly simplicity of character which has always been the best representative of the military profession. In higher regions it is otherwise, for the higher a man's rank, the more he must look around him; then arise interests on every side, and a manifold activity of the passions of good and bad. Envy and generosity, pride and humility, fierceness and tenderness, all may appear as active powers in this great drama.

21. PECULIARITY OF MIND.

The peculiar characteristics of mind in the chief actor have, as well as those of the feelings, a high importance. From an imaginative, flighty, inexperienced head, and from a calm, sagacious understanding, different things are to be expected.

22. FROM THE DIVERSITY IN MENTAL INDIVIDUALITIES ARISES THE DIVERSITY OF WAYS LEADING TO THE END.

It is this great diversity in mental individuality, the influence of which is to be supposed as chiefly felt in the higher ranks, because it increases as we progress upwards, which chiefly produces the diversity of ways leading to the end noticed by us in the first book, and which gives, to the play of probabilities and chance, such an unequal share in determining the course of events.

23. SECOND PECULIARITY.—LIVING REACTION.

The second peculiarity in War is the living reaction, and the reciprocal action resulting therefrom. We do not here speak of the difficulty of estimating that reaction, for that is included in the difficulty before mentioned, of treating the moral powers as quantities; but of this, that reciprocal action, by its nature, opposes anything like a regular plan. The effect which any measure produces upon the enemy is the most distinct of all the data which action affords; but every theory must keep to classes (or groups) of phenomena, and can never take up the really individual case in itself: that must everywhere be left to judgment and talent. It is therefore natural that in a business such as War, which in its plan—built upon general circumstances—is so often thwarted by unexpected and singular accidents, more must generally be left to talent; and less use can be made of a theoretical guide than in any other.

24. THIRD PECULIARITY.—UNCERTAINTY OF ALL DATA.

Lastly, the great uncertainty of all data in War is a peculiar difficulty, because all action must, to a certain extent, be planned in a mere twilight, which in addition not unfrequently—like the effect of a fog or moonshine—gives to things exaggerated dimensions and an unnatural appearance.

What this feeble light leaves indistinct to the sight talent must discover, or must be left to chance. It is therefore again talent, or the favour of fortune, on which reliance must be placed, for want of objective knowledge.

25. POSITIVE THEORY IS IMPOSSIBLE.

With materials of this kind we can only say to ourselves that it is a sheer impossibility to construct for the Art of War a theory which, like a scaffolding, shall ensure to the chief actor an external support on all sides. In all those cases in which he is thrown upon his talent he would find himself away from this scaffolding of theory and in opposition to it, and, however many-sided it might be framed, the same result would ensue of which we spoke when we said that talent and genius act beyond the law, and theory is in opposition to reality.

26. MEANS LEFT BY WHICH A THEORY IS POSSIBLE (THE DIFFICULTIES ARE NOT EVERYWHERE EQUALLY GREAT).

Two means present themselves of getting out of this difficulty. In the first place, what we have said of the nature of military action in general does not apply in the same manner to the action of every one, whatever may be his standing. In the lower ranks the spirit of self-sacrifice is called more into request, but the difficulties which the understanding and judgment meet with are infinitely less. The field of occurrences is more confined. Ends and means are fewer in number. Data more distinct; mostly also contained in the actually visible. But the higher we ascend the more the difficulties increase, until in the Commander-in-Chief they reach their climax, so that with him almost everything must be left to genius.

Further, according to a division of the subject in agreement with its nature, the difficulties are not everywhere the same, but diminish the more results manifest themselves in the material world, and increase the more they pass into the moral, and become motives which influence the will. Therefore it is easier to determine, by theoretical rules, the order and conduct of a battle, than the use to be made of the battle itself. Yonder physical weapons clash with each other, and although mind is not wanting therein, matter must have its rights. But in the effects to be produced by battles when the material results become motives, we have only to do with the moral nature. In a word, it is easier to make a theory for tactics than for strategy.

27. THEORY MUST BE OF THE NATURE OF OBSERVATIONS NOT OF DOCTRINE.

The second opening for the possibility of a theory lies in the point of view that it does not necessarily require to be a direction for action. As a general rule, whenever an activity is for the most part occupied with the same objects over and over again, with the same ends and means, although there may be trifling alterations and a corresponding number of varieties of combination, such things are capable of becoming a subject of study for the reasoning faculties. But such study is just the most essential part of every theory, and has a peculiar title to that name. It is an analytical investigation of the subject that leads to an exact knowledge; and if brought to bear on the results of experience, which in our case would be military history, to a thorough familiarity with it. The nearer theory attains the latter object, so much the more it passes over from the objective form of knowledge into the subjective one of skill in action; and so much the more, therefore, it will prove itself effective when circumstances allow of no other decision but that of personal talents; it will show its effects in that talent itself. If theory investigates the subjects which constitute War; if it separates more distinctly that which at first sight seems amalgamated; if it explains fully the properties of the means; if it shows their probable effects; if it makes evident the nature of objects; if it brings to bear all over the field of War the light of essentially critical investigation—then it has fulfilled the chief duties of its province. It becomes then a guide to him who wishes to make himself acquainted with War from books; it lights up the whole road for him, facilitates his progress, educates his judgment, and shields him from error.

If a man of expertness spends half his life in the endeavour to clear up an obscure subject thoroughly, he will probably know more about it than a person who seeks to master it in a short time. Theory is instituted that each person in succession may not have to go through the same labour of clearing the ground and toiling through his subject, but may find the thing in order, and light admitted on it. It should educate the mind of the future leader in War, or rather guide him in his self-instruction, but not accompany him to the field of battle; just as a sensible tutor forms and enlightens the opening mind of a youth without, therefore, keeping him in leading strings all through his life.

If maxims and rules result of themselves from the considerations which theory institutes, if the truth accretes itself into that form of crystal, then theory will not oppose this natural law of the mind; it will rather, if the arch ends in such a keystone, bring it prominently out; but so does this, only in order to satisfy the philosophical law of reason, in order to show distinctly the point to which the lines all converge, not in order to form out of it an algebraical formula for use upon the battle-field; for even these maxims and rules serve more to determine in the reflecting mind the leading outline of its habitual movements than as landmarks indicating to it the way in the act of execution.

28. BY THIS POINT OF VIEW THEORY BECOMES POSSIBLE, AND CEASES TO BE IN CONTRADICTION TO PRACTICE.

Taking this point of view, there is a possibility afforded of a satisfactory, that is, of a useful, theory of the conduct of War, never coming into opposition with the reality, and it will only depend on rational treatment to bring it so far into harmony with action that between theory and practice there shall no longer be that absurd difference which an unreasonable theory, in defiance of common sense, has often produced, but which, just as often, narrow-mindedness and ignorance have used as a pretext for giving way to their natural incapacity.

29. THEORY THEREFORE CONSIDERS THE NATURE OF ENDS AND MEANS—ENDS AND MEANS IN TACTICS.

Theory has therefore to consider the nature of the means and ends.

In tactics the means are the disciplined armed forces which are to carry on the contest. The object is victory. The precise definition of this conception can be better explained hereafter in the consideration of the combat. Here we content ourselves by denoting the retirement of the enemy from the field of battle as the sign of victory. By means of this victory strategy gains the object for which it appointed the combat, and which constitutes its special signification. This signification has certainly some influence on the nature of the victory. A victory which is intended to weaken the enemy's armed forces is a different thing from one which is designed only to put us in possession of a position. The signification of a combat may therefore have a sensible influence on the preparation and conduct of it, consequently will be also a subject of consideration in tactics.

30. CIRCUMSTANCES WHICH ALWAYS ATTEND THE APPLICATION OF THE MEANS.

As there are certain circumstances which attend the combat throughout, and have more or less influence upon its result, therefore these must be taken into consideration in the application of the armed forces.

These circumstances are the locality of the combat (ground), the time of day, and the weather.

31. LOCALITY.

The locality, which we prefer leaving for solution, under the head of "Country and Ground," might, strictly speaking, be without any influence at all if the combat took place on a completely level and uncultivated plain.

In a country of steppes such a case may occur, but in the cultivated countries of Europe it is almost an imaginary idea. Therefore a combat between civilised nations, in which country and ground have no influence, is hardly conceivable.

32. TIME OF DAY.

The time of day influences the combat by the difference between day and night; but the influence naturally extends further than merely to the limits of these divisions, as every combat has a certain duration, and great battles last for several hours. In the preparations for a great battle, it makes an essential difference whether it begins in the morning or the evening. At the same time, certainly many battles may be fought in which the question of the time of day is quite immaterial, and in the generality of cases its influence is only trifling.

33. WEATHER.

Still more rarely has the weather any decisive influence, and it is mostly only by fogs that it plays a part.

34. END AND MEANS IN STRATEGY.

Strategy has in the first instance only the victory, that is, the tactical result, as a means to its object, and ultimately those things which lead directly to peace. The application of its means to this object is at the same time attended by circumstances which have an influence thereon more or less.

35. CIRCUMSTANCES WHICH ATTEND THE APPLICATION OF THE MEANS OF STRATEGY.

These circumstances are country and ground, the former including the territory and inhabitants of the whole theatre of war; next the time of the day, and the time of the year as well; lastly, the weather, particularly any unusual state of the same, severe frost, &c.

36. THESE FORM NEW MEANS.

By bringing these things into combination with the results of a combat, strategy gives this result—and therefore the combat—a special signification, places before it a particular object. But when this object is not that which leads directly to peace, therefore a subordinate one, it is only to be looked upon as a means; and therefore in strategy we may look upon the results of combats or victories, in all their different significations, as means. The conquest of a position is such a result of a combat applied to ground. But not only are the different combats with special objects to be considered as means, but also every higher aim which we may have in view in the combination of battles directed on a common object is to be regarded as a means. A winter campaign is a combination of this kind applied to the season.

There remain, therefore, as objects, only those things which may be supposed as leading directly to peace, Theory investigates all these ends and means according to the nature of their effects and their mutual relations.

37. STRATEGY DEDUCES ONLY FROM EXPERIENCE THE ENDS AND MEANS TO BE EXAMINED.

The first question is, How does strategy arrive at a complete list of these things? If there is to be a philosophical inquiry leading to an absolute result, it would become entangled in all those difficulties which the logical necessity of the conduct of War and its theory exclude. It therefore turns to experience, and directs its attention on those combinations which military history can furnish. In this manner, no doubt, nothing more than a limited theory can be obtained, which only suits circumstances such as are presented in history. But this incompleteness is unavoidable, because in any case theory must either have deduced from, or have compared with, history what it advances with respect to things. Besides, this incompleteness in every case is more theoretical than real.

One great advantage of this method is that theory cannot lose itself in abstruse disquisitions, subtleties, and chimeras, but must always remain practical.

38. HOW FAR THE ANALYSIS OF THE MEANS SHOULD BE CARRIED.

Another question is, How far should theory go in its analysis of the means? Evidently only so far as the elements in a separate form present themselves for consideration in practice. The range and effect of different weapons is very important to tactics; their construction, although these effects result from it, is a matter of indifference; for the conduct of War is not making powder and cannon out of a given quantity of charcoal, sulphur, and saltpetre, of copper and tin: the given quantities for the conduct of War are arms in a finished state and their effects. Strategy makes use of maps without troubling itself about triangulations; it does not inquire how the country is subdivided into departments and provinces, and how the people are educated and governed, in order to attain the best military results; but it takes things as it finds them in the community of European States, and observes where very different conditions have a notable influence on War.

39. GREAT SIMPLIFICATION OF THE KNOWLEDGE REQUIRED.

That in this manner the number of subjects for theory is much simplified, and the knowledge requisite for the conduct of War much reduced, is easy to perceive. The very great mass of knowledge and appliances of skill which minister to the action of War in general, and which are necessary before an army fully equipped can take the field, unite in a few great results before they are able to reach, in actual War, the final goal of their activity; just as the streams of a country unite themselves in rivers before they fall into the sea. Only those activities emptying themselves directly into the sea of War have to be studied by him who is to conduct its operations.

40. THIS EXPLAINS THE RAPID GROWTH OF GREAT GENERALS, AND WHY A GENERAL IS NOT A MAN OF LEARNING.

This result of our considerations is in fact so necessary, any other would have made us distrustful of their accuracy. Only thus is explained how so often men have made their appearance with great success in War, and indeed in the higher ranks even in supreme Command, whose pursuits had been previously of a totally different nature; indeed how, as a rule, the most distinguished Generals have never risen from the very learned or really erudite class of officers, but have been mostly men who, from the circumstances of their position, could not have attained to any great amount of knowledge. On that account those who have considered it necessary or even beneficial to commence the education of a future General by instruction in all details have always been ridiculed as absurd pedants. It would be easy to show the injurious tendency of such a course, because the human mind is trained by the knowledge imparted to it and the direction given to its ideas. Only what is great can make it great; the little can only make it little, if the mind itself does not reject it as something repugnant.

41. FORMER CONTRADICTIONS.

Because this simplicity of knowledge requisite in War was not attended to, but that knowledge was always jumbled up with the whole impedimenta of subordinate sciences and arts, therefore the palpable opposition to the events of real life which resulted could not be solved otherwise than by ascribing it all to genius, which requires no theory and for which no theory could be prescribed.

42. ON THIS ACCOUNT ALL USE OF KNOWLEDGE WAS DENIED, AND EVERYTHING ASCRIBED TO NATURAL TALENTS.

People with whom common sense had the upper hand felt sensible of the immense distance remaining to be filled up between a genius of the highest order and a learned pedant; and they became in a manner free-thinkers, rejected all belief in theory, and affirmed the conduct of War to be a natural function of man, which he performs more or less well according as he has brought with him into the world more or less talent in that direction. It cannot be denied that these were nearer to the truth than those who placed a value on false knowledge: at the same time it may easily be seen that such a view is itself but an exaggeration. No activity of the human understanding is possible without a certain stock of ideas; but these are, for the greater part at least, not innate but acquired, and constitute his knowledge. The only question therefore is, of what kind should these ideas be; and we think we have answered it if we say that they should be directed on those things which man has directly to deal with in War.

43. THE KNOWLEDGE MUST BE MADE SUITABLE TO THE POSITION.

Inside this field itself of military activity, the knowledge required must be different according to the station of the Commander. It will be directed on smaller and more circumscribed objects if he holds an inferior, upon greater and more comprehensive ones if he holds a higher situation. There are Field Marshals who would not have shone at the head of a cavalry regiment, and vice versa.

44. THE KNOWLEDGE IN WAR IS VERY SIMPLE, BUT NOT, AT THE SAME TIME, VERY EASY.

But although the knowledge in War is simple, that is to say directed to so few subjects, and taking up those only in their final results, the art of execution is not, on that account, easy. Of the difficulties to which activity in War is subject generally, we have already spoken in the first book; we here omit those things which can only be overcome by courage, and maintain also that the activity of mind, is only simple, and easy in inferior stations, but increases in difficulty with increase of rank, and in the highest position, in that of Commander-in-Chief, is to be reckoned among the most difficult which there is for the human mind.

45. OF THE NATURE OF THIS KNOWLEDGE.

The Commander of an Army neither requires to be a learned explorer of history nor a publicist, but he must be well versed in the higher affairs of State; he must know, and be able to judge correctly of traditional tendencies, interests at stake, the immediate questions at issue, and the characters of leading persons; he need not be a close observer of men, a sharp dissector of human character, but he must know the character, the feelings, the habits, the peculiar faults and inclinations of those whom he is to command. He need not understand anything about the make of a carriage, or the harness of a battery horse, but he must know how to calculate exactly the march of a column, under different circumstances, according to the time it requires. These are matters the knowledge of which cannot be forced out by an apparatus of scientific formula and machinery: they are only to be gained by the exercise of an accurate judgment in the observation of things and of men, aided by a special talent for the apprehension of both.

The necessary knowledge for a high position in military action is therefore distinguished by this, that by observation, therefore by study and reflection, it is only to be attained through a special talent which as an intellectual instinct understands how to extract from the phenomena of life only the essence or spirit, as bees do the honey from the flowers; and that it is also to be gained by experience of life as well as by study and reflection. Life will never bring forth a Newton or an Euler by its rich teachings, but it may bring forth great calculators in War, such as Condé or Frederick.

It is therefore not necessary that, in order to vindicate the intellectual dignity of military activity, we should resort to untruth and silly pedantry. There never has been a great and distinguished Commander of contracted mind, but very numerous are the instances of men who, after serving with the greatest distinction in inferior positions, remained below mediocrity in the highest, from insufficiency of intellectual capacity. That even amongst those holding the post of Commander-in-Chief there may be a difference according to the degree of their plenitude of power is a matter of course.

46. SCIENCE MUST BECOME ART.

Now we have yet to consider one condition which is more necessary for the knowledge of the conduct of War than for any other, which is, that it must pass completely into the mind and almost completely cease to be something objective. In almost all other arts and occupations of life the active agent can make use of truths which he has only learnt once, and in the spirit and sense of which he no longer lives, and which he extracts from dusty books. Even truths which he has in hand and uses daily may continue something external to himself, If the architect takes up a pen to settle the strength of a pier by a complicated calculation, the truth found as a result is no emanation from his own mind. He had first to find the data with labour, and then to submit these to an operation of the mind, the rule for which he did not discover, the necessity of which he is perhaps at the moment only partly conscious of, but which he applies, for the most part, as if by mechanical dexterity. But it is never so in War. The moral reaction, the ever-changeful form of things, makes it necessary for the chief actor to carry in himself the whole mental apparatus of his knowledge, that anywhere and at every pulse-beat he may be capable of giving the requisite decision from himself. Knowledge must, by this complete assimilation with his own mind and life, be converted into real power. This is the reason why everything seems so easy with men distinguished in War, and why everything is ascribed to natural talent. We say natural talent, in order thereby to distinguish it from that which is formed and matured by observation and study.

We think that by these reflections we have explained the problem of a theory of the conduct of War; and pointed out the way to its solution.

Of the two fields into which we have divided the conduct of War, tactics and strategy, the theory of the latter contains unquestionably, as before observed, the greatest difficulties, because the first is almost limited to a circumscribed field of objects, but the latter, in the direction of objects leading directly to peace, opens to itself an unlimited field of possibilities. Since for the most part the Commander-in-Chief has only to keep these objects steadily in view, therefore the part of strategy in which he moves is also that which is particularly subject to this difficulty.

Theory, therefore, especially where it comprehends the highest services, will stop much sooner in strategy than in tactics at the simple consideration of things, and content itself to assist the Commander to that insight into things which, blended with his whole thought, makes his course easier and surer, never forces him into opposition with himself in order to obey an objective truth.

CHAPTER III. Art or Science of War

1.—USAGE STILL UNSETTLED

(POWER AND KNOWLEDGE. SCIENCE WHEN MERE KNOWING; ART, WHEN DOING, IS THE OBJECT.)

The choice between these terms seems to be still unsettled, and no one seems to know rightly on what grounds it should be decided, and yet the thing is simple. We have already said elsewhere that "knowing" is something different from "doing." The two are so different that they should not easily be mistaken the one for the other. The "doing" cannot properly stand in any book, and therefore also Art should never be the title of a book. But because we have once accustomed ourselves to combine in conception, under the name of theory of Art, or simply Art, the branches of knowledge (which may be separately pure sciences) necessary for the practice of an Art, therefore it is consistent to continue this ground of distinction, and to call everything Art when the object is to carry out the "doing" (being able), as for example, Art of building; Science, when merely knowledge is the object; as Science of mathematics, of astronomy. That in every Art certain complete sciences may be included is intelligible of itself, and should not perplex us. But still it is worth observing that there is also no science without a mixture of Art. In mathematics, for instance, the use of figures and of algebra is an Art, but that is only one amongst many instances. The reason is, that however plain and palpable the difference is between knowledge and power in the composite results of human knowledge, yet it is difficult to trace out their line of separation in man himself.

2. DIFFICULTY OF SEPARATING PERCEPTION FROM JUDGMENT.

(ART OF WAR.)

All thinking is indeed Art. Where the logician draws the line, where the premises stop which are the result of cognition—where judgment begins, there Art begins. But more than this even the perception of the mind is judgment again, and consequently Art; and at last, even the perception by the senses as well. In a word, if it is impossible to imagine a human being possessing merely the faculty of cognition, devoid of judgment or the reverse, so also Art and Science can never be completely separated from each other. The more these subtle elements of light embody themselves in the outward forms of the world, so much the more separate appear their domains; and now once more, where the object is creation and production, there is the province of Art; where the object is investigation and knowledge Science holds sway.—After all this it results of itself that it is more fitting to say Art of War than Science of War.

So much for this, because we cannot do without these conceptions. But now we come forward with the assertion that War is neither an Art nor a Science in the real signification, and that it is just the setting out from that starting-point of ideas which has led to a wrong direction being taken, which has caused War to be put on a par with other arts and sciences, and has led to a number of erroneous analogies.

This has indeed been felt before now, and on that it was maintained that War is a handicraft; but there was more lost than gained by that, for a handicraft is only an inferior art, and as such is also subject to definite and rigid laws. In reality the Art of War did go on for some time in the spirit of a handicraft—we allude to the times of the Condottieri—but then it received that direction, not from intrinsic but from external causes; and military history shows how little it was at that time in accordance with the nature of the thing.

3. WAR IS PART OF THE INTERCOURSE OF THE HUMAN RACE.

We say therefore War belongs not to the province of Arts and Sciences, but to the province of social life. It is a conflict of great interests which is settled by bloodshed, and only in that is it different from others. It would be better, instead of comparing it with any Art, to liken it to business competition, which is also a conflict of human interests and activities; and it is still more like State policy, which again, on its part, may be looked upon as a kind of business competition on a great scale. Besides, State policy is the womb in which War is developed, in which its outlines lie hidden in a rudimentary state, like the qualities of living creatures in their germs.(*)

(*) The analogy has become much closer since Clausewitz's time. Now that the first business of the State is regarded as the development of facilities for trade, War between great nations is only a question of time. No Hague Conferences can avert it—EDITOR.

4. DIFFERENCE.

The essential difference consists in this, that War is no activity of the will, which exerts itself upon inanimate matter like the mechanical Arts; or upon a living but still passive and yielding subject, like the human mind and the human feelings in the ideal Arts, but against a living and reacting force. How little the categories of Arts and Sciences are applicable to such an activity strikes us at once; and we can understand at the same time how that constant seeking and striving after laws like those which may be developed out of the dead material world could not but lead to constant errors. And yet it is just the mechanical Arts that some people would imitate in the Art of War. The imitation of the ideal Arts was quite out of the question, because these themselves dispense too much with laws and rules, and those hitherto tried, always acknowledged as insufficient and one-sided, are perpetually undermined and washed away by the current of opinions, feelings, and customs.

Whether such a conflict of the living, as takes place and is settled in War, is subject to general laws, and whether these are capable of indicating a useful line of action, will be partly investigated in this book; but so much is evident in itself, that this, like every other subject which does not surpass our powers of understanding, may be lighted up, and be made more or less plain in its inner relations by an inquiring mind, and that alone is sufficient to realise the idea of a THEORY.

CHAPTER IV. Methodicism

In order to explain ourselves clearly as to the conception of method, and method of action, which play such an important part in War, we must be allowed to cast a hasty glance at the logical hierarchy through which, as through regularly constituted official functionaries, the world of action is governed.

Law, in the widest sense strictly applying to perception as well as action, has plainly something subjective and arbitrary in its literal meaning, and expresses just that on which we and those things external to us are dependent. As a subject of cognition, Law is the relation of things and their effects to one another; as a subject of the will, it is a motive of action, and is then equivalent to command or prohibition.

Principle is likewise such a law for action, except that it has not the formal definite meaning, but is only the spirit and sense of law in order to leave the judgment more freedom of application when the diversity of the real world cannot be laid hold of under the definite form of a law. As the judgment must of itself suggest the cases in which the principle is not applicable, the latter therefore becomes in that way a real aid or guiding star for the person acting.

Principle is objective when it is the result of objective truth, and consequently of equal value for all men; it is subjective, and then generally called maxim if there are subjective relations in it, and if it therefore has a certain value only for the person himself who makes it.

Rule is frequently taken in the sense of Law, and then means the same as Principle, for we say “no rule without exceptions,” but we do not say “no law without exceptions,” a sign that with Rule we retain to ourselves more freedom of application.

In another meaning Rule is the means used of discerning a recondite truth in a particular sign lying close at hand, in order to attach to this particular sign the law of action directed upon the whole truth. Of this kind are all the rules of games of play, all abridged processes in mathematics, &c.

Directions and instructions are determinations of action which have an influence upon a number of minor circumstances too numerous and unimportant for general laws.

Lastly, Method, mode of acting, is an always recurring proceeding selected out of several possible ones; and Methodicism (METHODISMUS) is that which is determined by methods instead of by general principles or particular prescriptions. By this the cases which are placed under such methods must necessarily be supposed alike in their essential parts. As they cannot all be this, then the point is that at least as many as possible should be; in other words, that Method should be calculated on the most probable cases. Methodicism is therefore not founded on determined particular premises, but on the average probability of cases one with another; and its ultimate tendency is to set up an average truth, the constant and uniform, application of which soon acquires something of the nature of a mechanical appliance, which in the end does that which is right almost unwittingly.

The conception of law in relation to perception is not necessary for the conduct of War, because the complex phenomena of War are not so regular, and the regular are not so complex, that we should gain anything more by this conception than by the simple truth. And where a simple conception and language is sufficient, to resort to the complex becomes affected and pedantic. The conception of law in relation to action cannot be used in the theory of the conduct of War, because owing to the variableness and diversity of the phenomena there is in it no determination of such a general nature as to deserve the name of law.

But principles, rules, prescriptions, and methods are conceptions indispensable to a theory of the conduct of War, in so far as that theory leads to positive doctrines, because in doctrines the truth can only crystallise itself in such forms.

As tactics is the branch of the conduct of War in which theory can attain the nearest to positive doctrine, therefore these conceptions will appear in it most frequently.

Not to use cavalry against unbroken infantry except in some case of special emergency, only to use firearms within effective range in the combat, to spare the forces as much as possible for the final struggle—these are tactical principles. None of them can be applied absolutely in every case, but they must always be present to the mind of the Chief, in order that the benefit of the truth contained in them may not be lost in cases where that truth can be of advantage.

If from the unusual cooking by an enemy's camp his movement is inferred, if the intentional exposure of troops in a combat indicates a false attack, then this way of discerning the truth is called rule, because from a single visible circumstance that conclusion is drawn which corresponds with the same.

If it is a rule to attack the enemy with renewed vigour, as soon as he begins to limber up his artillery in the combat, then on this particular fact depends a course of action which is aimed at the general situation of the enemy as inferred from the above fact, namely, that he is about to give up the fight, that he is commencing to draw off his troops, and is neither capable of making a serious stand while thus drawing off nor of making his retreat gradually in good order.

Regulations and methods bring preparatory theories into the conduct of War, in so far as disciplined troops are inoculated with them as active principles. The whole body of instructions for formations, drill, and field service are regulations and methods: in the drill instructions the first predominate, in the field service instructions the latter. To these things the real conduct of War attaches itself; it takes them over, therefore, as given modes of proceeding, and as such they must appear in the theory of the conduct of War.

But for those activities retaining freedom in the employment of these forces there cannot be regulations, that is, definite instructions, because they would do away with freedom of action. Methods, on the other hand, as a general way of executing duties as they arise, calculated, as we have said, on an average of probability, or as a dominating influence of principles and rules carried through to application, may certainly appear in the theory of the conduct of War, provided only they are not represented as something different from what they are, not as the absolute and necessary modes of action (systems), but as the best of general forms which may be used as shorter ways in place of a particular disposition for the occasion, at discretion.

But the frequent application of methods will be seen to be most essential and unavoidable in the conduct of War, if we reflect how much action proceeds on mere conjecture, or in complete uncertainty, because one side is prevented from learning all the circumstances which influence the dispositions of the other, or because, even if these circumstances which influence the decisions of the one were really known, there is not, owing to their extent and the dispositions they would entail, sufficient time for the other to carry out all necessary counteracting measures—that therefore measures in War must always be calculated on a certain number of possibilities; if we reflect how numberless are the trifling things belonging to any single event, and which therefore should be taken into account along with it, and that therefore there is no other means to suppose the one counteracted by the other, and to base our arrangements only upon what is of a general nature and probable; if we reflect lastly that, owing to the increasing number of officers as we descend the scale of rank, less must be left to the true discernment and ripe judgment of individuals the lower the sphere of action, and that when we reach those ranks where we can look for no other notions but those which the regulations of the service and experience afford, we must help them with the methodic forms bordering on those regulations. This will serve both as a support to their judgment and a barrier against those extravagant and erroneous views which are so especially to be dreaded in a sphere where experience is so costly.

Besides this absolute need of method in action, we must also acknowledge that it has a positive advantage, which is that, through the constant repetition of a formal exercise, a readiness, precision, and firmness is attained in the movement of troops which diminishes the natural friction, and makes the machine move easier.

Method will therefore be the more generally used, become the more indispensable, the farther down the scale of rank the position of the active agent; and on the other hand, its use will diminish upwards, until in the highest position it quite disappears. For this reason it is more in its place in tactics than in strategy.

War in its highest aspects consists not of an infinite number of little events, the diversities in which compensate each other, and which therefore by a better or worse method are better or worse governed, but of separate great decisive events which must be dealt with separately. It is not like a field of stalks, which, without any regard to the particular form of each stalk, will be mowed better or worse, according as the mowing instrument is good or bad, but rather as a group of large trees, to which the axe must be laid with judgment, according to the particular form and inclination of each separate trunk.

How high up in military activity the admissibility of method in action reaches naturally determines itself, not according to actual rank, but according to things; and it affects the highest positions in a less degree, only because these positions have the most comprehensive subjects of activity. A constant order of battle, a constant formation of advance guards and outposts, are methods by which a General ties not only his subordinates' hands, but also his own in certain cases. Certainly they may have been devised by himself, and may be applied by him according to circumstances, but they may also be a subject of theory, in so far as they are based on the general properties of troops and weapons. On the other hand, any method by which definite plans for wars or campaigns are to be given out all ready made as if from a machine are absolutely worthless.

As long as there exists no theory which can be sustained, that is, no enlightened treatise on the conduct of War, method in action cannot but encroach beyond its proper limits in high places, for men employed in these spheres of activity have not always had the opportunity of educating themselves, through study and through contact with the higher interests. In the impracticable and inconsistent disquisitions of theorists and critics they cannot find their way, their sound common sense rejects them, and as they bring with them no knowledge but that derived from experience, therefore in those cases which admit of, and require, a free individual treatment they readily make use of the means which experience gives them—that is, an imitation of the particular methods practised by great Generals, by which a method of action then arises of itself. If we see Frederick the Great's Generals always making their appearance in the so-called oblique order of battle, the Generals of the French Revolution always using turning movements with a long, extended line of battle, and Buonaparte's lieutenants rushing to the attack with the bloody energy of concentrated masses, then we recognise in the recurrence of the mode of proceeding evidently an adopted method, and see therefore that method of action can reach up to regions bordering on the highest. Should an improved theory facilitate the study of the conduct of War, form the mind and judgment of men who are rising to the highest commands, then also method in action will no longer reach so far, and so much of it as is to be considered indispensable will then at least be formed from theory itself, and not take place out of mere imitation. However pre-eminently a great Commander does things, there is always something subjective in the way he does them; and if he has a certain manner, a large share of his individuality is contained in it which does not always accord with the individuality of the person who copies his manner.

At the same time, it would neither be possible nor right to banish subjective methodicism or manner completely from the conduct of War: it is rather to be regarded as a manifestation of that influence which the general character of a War has upon its separate events, and to which satisfaction can only be done in that way if theory is not able to foresee this general character and include it in its considerations. What is more natural than that the War of the French Revolution had its own way of doing things? and what theory could ever have included that peculiar method? The evil is only that such a manner originating in a special case easily outlives itself, because it continues whilst circumstances imperceptibly change. This is what theory should prevent by lucid and rational criticism. When in the year 1806 the Prussian Generals, Prince Louis at Saalfeld, Tauentzien on the Dornberg near Jena, Grawert before and Ruechel behind Kappellendorf, all threw themselves into the open jaws of destruction in the oblique order of Frederick the Great, and managed to ruin Hohenlohe's Army in a way that no Army was ever ruined, even on the field of battle, all this was done through a manner which had outlived its day, together with the most downright stupidity to which methodicism ever led.

CHAPTER V. Criticism

The influence of theoretical principles upon real life is produced more through criticism than through doctrine, for as criticism is an application of abstract truth to real events, therefore it not only brings truth of this description nearer to life, but also accustoms the understanding more to such truths by the constant repetition of their application. We therefore think it necessary to fix the point of view for criticism next to that for theory.

From the simple narration of an historical occurrence which places events in chronological order, or at most only touches on their more immediate causes, we separate the CRITICAL.

In this CRITICAL three different operations of the mind may be observed.

First, the historical investigation and determining of doubtful facts. This is properly historical research, and has nothing in common with theory.

Secondly, the tracing of effects to causes. This is the REAL CRITICAL INQUIRY; it is indispensable to theory, for everything which in theory is to be established, supported, or even merely explained, by experience can only be settled in this way.

Thirdly, the testing of the means employed. This is criticism, properly speaking, in which praise and censure is contained. This is where theory helps history, or rather, the teaching to be derived from it.

In these two last strictly critical parts of historical study, all depends on tracing things to their primary elements, that is to say, up to undoubted truths, and not, as is so often done, resting half-way, that is, on some arbitrary assumption or supposition.

As respects the tracing of effect to cause, that is often attended with the insuperable difficulty that the real causes are not known. In none of the relations of life does this so frequently happen as in War, where events are seldom fully known, and still less motives, as the latter have been, perhaps purposely, concealed by the chief actor, or have been of such a transient and accidental character that they have been lost for history. For this reason critical narration must generally proceed hand in hand with historical investigation, and still such a want of connection between cause and effect will often present itself, that it does not seem justifiable to consider effects as the necessary results of known causes. Here, therefore must occur, that is, historical results which cannot be made use of for teaching. All that theory can demand is that the investigation should be rigidly conducted up to that point, and there leave off without drawing conclusions. A real evil springs up only if the known is made perforce to suffice as an explanation of effects, and thus a false importance is ascribed to it.

Besides this difficulty, critical inquiry also meets with another great and intrinsic one, which is that the progress of events in War seldom proceeds from one simple cause, but from several in common, and that it therefore is not sufficient to follow up a series of events to their origin in a candid and impartial spirit, but that it is then also necessary to apportion to each contributing cause its due weight. This leads, therefore, to a closer investigation of their nature, and thus a critical investigation may lead into what is the proper field of theory.

The critical CONSIDERATION, that is, the testing of the means, leads to the question, Which are the effects peculiar to the means applied, and whether these effects were comprehended in the plans of the person directing?

The effects peculiar to the means lead to the investigation of their nature, and thus again into the field of theory.

We have already seen that in criticism all depends upon attaining to positive truth; therefore, that we must not stop at arbitrary propositions which are not allowed by others, and to which other perhaps equally arbitrary assertions may again be opposed, so that there is no end to pros and cons; the whole is without result, and therefore without instruction.

We have seen that both the search for causes and the examination of means lead into the field of theory; that is, into the field of universal truth, which does not proceed solely from the case immediately under examination. If there is a theory which can be used, then the critical consideration will appeal to the proofs there afforded, and the examination may there stop.

But where no such theoretical truth is to be found, the inquiry must be pushed up to the original elements. If this necessity occurs often, it must lead the historian (according to a common expression) into a labyrinth of details. He then has his hands full, and it is impossible for him to stop to give the requisite attention everywhere; the consequence is, that in order to set bounds to his investigation, he adopts some arbitrary assumptions which, if they do not appear so to him, do so to others, as they are not evident in themselves or capable of proof.

A sound theory is therefore an essential foundation for criticism, and it is impossible for it, without the assistance of a sensible theory, to attain to that point at which it commences chiefly to be instructive, that is, where it becomes demonstration, both convincing and sans réplique.

But it would be a visionary hope to believe in the possibility of a theory applicable to every abstract truth, leaving nothing for criticism to do but to place the case under its appropriate law: it would be ridiculous pedantry to lay down as a rule for criticism that it must always halt and turn round on reaching the boundaries of sacred theory. The same spirit of analytical inquiry which is the origin of theory must also guide the critic in his work; and it can and must therefore happen that he strays beyond the boundaries of the province of theory and elucidates those points with which he is more particularly concerned. It is more likely, on the contrary, that criticism would completely fail in its object if it degenerated into a mechanical application of theory. All positive results of theoretical inquiry, all principles, rules, and methods, are the more wanting in generality and positive truth the more they become positive doctrine. They exist to offer themselves for use as required, and it must always be left for judgment to decide whether they are suitable or not. Such results of theory must never be used in criticism as rules or norms for a standard, but in the same way as the person acting should use them, that is, merely as aids to judgment. If it is an acknowledged principle in tactics that in the usual order of battle cavalry should be placed behind infantry, not in line with it, still it would be folly on this account to condemn every deviation from this principle. Criticism must investigate the grounds of the deviation, and it is only in case these are insufficient that it has a right to appeal to principles laid down in theory. If it is further established in theory that a divided attack diminishes the probability of success, still it would be just as unreasonable, whenever there is a divided attack and an unsuccessful issue, to regard the latter as the result of the former, without further investigation into the connection between the two, as where a divided attack is successful to infer from it the fallacy of that theoretical principle. The spirit of investigation which belongs to criticism cannot allow either. Criticism therefore supports itself chiefly on the results of the analytical investigation of theory; what has been made out and determined by theory does not require to be demonstrated over again by criticism, and it is so determined by theory that criticism may find it ready demonstrated.

This office of criticism, of examining the effect produced by certain causes, and whether a means applied has answered its object, will be easy enough if cause and effect, means and end, are all near together.

If an Army is surprised, and therefore cannot make a regular and intelligent use of its powers and resources, then the effect of the surprise is not doubtful.—If theory has determined that in a battle the convergent form of attack is calculated to produce greater but less certain results, then the question is whether he who employs that convergent form had in view chiefly that greatness of result as his object; if so, the proper means were chosen. But if by this form he intended to make the result more certain, and that expectation was founded not on some exceptional circumstances (in this case), but on the general nature of the convergent form, as has happened a hundred times, then he mistook the nature of the means and committed an error.

Here the work of military investigation and criticism is easy, and it will always be so when confined to the immediate effects and objects. This can be done quite at option, if we abstract the connection of the parts with the whole, and only look at things in that relation.

But in War, as generally in the world, there is a connection between everything which belongs to a whole; and therefore, however small a cause may be in itself, its effects reach to the end of the act of warfare, and modify or influence the final result in some degree, let that degree be ever so small. In the same manner every means must be felt up to the ultimate object.

We can therefore trace the effects of a cause as long as events are worth noticing, and in the same way we must not stop at the testing of a means for the immediate object, but test also this object as a means to a higher one, and thus ascend the series of facts in succession, until we come to one so absolutely necessary in its nature as to require no examination or proof. In many cases, particularly in what concerns great and decisive measures, the investigation must be carried to the final aim, to that which leads immediately to peace.

It is evident that in thus ascending, at every new station which we reach a new point of view for the judgment is attained, so that the same means which appeared advisable at one station, when looked at from the next above it may have to be rejected.

The search for the causes of events and the comparison of means with ends must always go hand in hand in the critical review of an act, for the investigation of causes leads us first to the discovery of those things which are worth examining.

This following of the clue up and down is attended with considerable difficulty, for the farther from an event the cause lies which we are looking for, the greater must be the number of other causes which must at the same time be kept in view and allowed for in reference to the share which they have in the course of events, and then eliminated, because the higher the importance of a fact the greater will be the number of separate forces and circumstances by which it is conditioned. If we have unravelled the causes of a battle being lost, we have certainly also ascertained a part of the causes of the consequences which this defeat has upon the whole War, but only a part, because the effects of other causes, more or less according to circumstances, will flow into the final result.

The same multiplicity of circumstances is presented also in the examination of the means the higher our point of view, for the higher the object is situated, the greater must be the number of means employed to reach it. The ultimate object of the War is the object aimed at by all the Armies simultaneously, and it is therefore necessary that the consideration should embrace all that each has done or could have done.

It is obvious that this may sometimes lead to a wide field of inquiry, in which it is easy to wander and lose the way, and in which this difficulty prevails—that a number of assumptions or suppositions must be made about a variety of things which do not actually appear, but which in all probability did take place, and therefore cannot possibly be left out of consideration.

When Buonaparte, in 1797, at the head of the Army of Italy, advanced from the Tagliamento against the Archduke Charles, he did so with a view to force that General to a decisive action before the reinforcements expected from the Rhine had reached him. If we look, only at the immediate object, the means were well chosen and justified by the result, for the Archduke was so inferior in numbers that he only made a show of resistance on the Tagliamento, and when he saw his adversary so strong and resolute, yielded ground, and left open the passages, of the Norican Alps. Now to what use could Buonaparte turn this fortunate event? To penetrate into the heart of the Austrian empire itself, to facilitate the advance of the Rhine Armies under Moreau and Hoche, and open communication with them? This was the view taken by Buonaparte, and from this point of view he was right. But now, if criticism places itself at a higher point of view—namely, that of the French Directory, which body could see and know that the Armies on the Rhine could not commence the campaign for six weeks, then the advance of Buonaparte over the Norican Alps can only be regarded as an extremely hazardous measure; for if the Austrians had drawn largely on their Rhine Armies to reinforce their Army in Styria, so as to enable the Archduke to fall upon the Army of Italy, not only would that Army have been routed, but the whole campaign lost. This consideration, which attracted the serious attention of Buonaparte at Villach, no doubt induced him to sign the armistice of Leoben with so much readiness.

If criticism takes a still higher position, and if it knows that the Austrians had no reserves between the Army of the Archduke Charles and Vienna, then we see that Vienna became threatened by the advance of the Army of Italy.

Supposing that Buonaparte knew that the capital was thus uncovered, and knew that he still retained the same superiority in numbers over the Archduke as he had in Styria, then his advance against the heart of the Austrian States was no longer without purpose, and its value depended on the value which the Austrians might place on preserving their capital. If that was so great that, rather than lose it, they would accept the conditions of peace which Buonaparte was ready to offer them, it became an object of the first importance to threaten Vienna. If Buonaparte had any reason to know this, then criticism may stop there, but if this point was only problematical, then criticism must take a still higher position, and ask what would have followed if the Austrians had resolved to abandon Vienna and retire farther into the vast dominions still left to them. But it is easy to see that this question cannot be answered without bringing into the consideration the probable movements of the Rhine Armies on both sides. Through the decided superiority of numbers on the side of the French—130,000 to 80,000—there could be little doubt of the result; but then next arises the question, What use would the Directory make of a victory; whether they would follow up their success to the opposite frontiers of the Austrian monarchy, therefore to the complete breaking up or overthrow of that power, or whether they would be satisfied with the conquest of a considerable portion to serve as a security for peace? The probable result in each case must be estimated, in order to come to a conclusion as to the probable determination of the Directory. Supposing the result of these considerations to be that the French forces were much too weak for the complete subjugation of the Austrian monarchy, so that the attempt might completely reverse the respective positions of the contending Armies, and that even the conquest and occupation of a considerable district of country would place the French Army in strategic relations to which they were not equal, then that result must naturally influence the estimate of the position of the Army of Italy, and compel it to lower its expectations. And this, it was no doubt which influenced Buonaparte, although fully aware of the helpless condition of the Archduke, still to sign the peace of Campo Formio, which imposed no greater sacrifices on the Austrians than the loss of provinces which, even if the campaign took the most favourable turn for them, they could not have reconquered. But the French could not have reckoned on even the moderate treaty of Campo Formio, and therefore it could not have been their object in making their bold advance if two considerations had not presented themselves to their view, the first of which consisted in the question, what degree of value the Austrians would attach to each of the above-mentioned results; whether, notwithstanding the probability of a satisfactory result in either of these cases, would it be worth while to make the sacrifices inseparable from a continuance of the War, when they could be spared those sacrifices by a peace on terms not too humiliating? The second consideration is the question whether the Austrian Government, instead of seriously weighing the possible results of a resistance pushed to extremities, would not prove completely disheartened by the impression of their present reverses.

The consideration which forms the subject of the first is no idle piece of subtle argument, but a consideration of such decidedly practical importance that it comes up whenever the plan of pushing War to the utmost extremity is mooted, and by its weight in most cases restrains the execution of such plans.

The second consideration is of equal importance, for we do not make War with an abstraction but with a reality, which we must always keep in view, and we may be sure that it was not overlooked by the bold Buonaparte—that is, that he was keenly alive to the terror which the appearance of his sword inspired. It was reliance on that which led him to Moscow. There it led him into a scrape. The terror of him had been weakened by the gigantic struggles in which he had been engaged; in the year 1797 it was still fresh, and the secret of a resistance pushed to extremities had not been discovered; nevertheless even in 1797 his boldness might have led to a negative result if, as already said, he had not with a sort of presentiment avoided it by signing the moderate peace of Campo Formio.

We must now bring these considerations to a close—they will suffice to show the wide sphere, the diversity and embarrassing nature of the subjects embraced in a critical examination carried to the fullest extent, that is, to those measures of a great and decisive class which must necessarily be included. It follows from them that besides a theoretical acquaintance with the subject, natural talent must also have a great influence on the value of critical examinations, for it rests chiefly with the latter to throw the requisite light on the interrelations of things, and to distinguish from amongst the endless connections of events those which are really essential.

But talent is also called into requisition in another way. Critical examination is not merely the appreciation of those means which have been actually employed, but also of all possible means, which therefore must be suggested in the first place—that is, must be discovered; and the use of any particular means is not fairly open to censure until a better is pointed out. Now, however small the number of possible combinations may be in most cases, still it must be admitted that to point out those which have not been used is not a mere analysis of actual things, but a spontaneous creation which cannot be prescribed, and depends on the fertility of genius.

We are far from seeing a field for great genius in a case which admits only of the application of a few simple combinations, and we think it exceedingly ridiculous to hold up, as is often done, the turning of a position as an invention showing the highest genius; still nevertheless this creative self-activity on the part of the critic is necessary, and it is one of the points which essentially determine the value of critical examination.

When Buonaparte on 30th July, 1796, determined to raise the siege of Mantua, in order to march with his whole force against the enemy, advancing in separate columns to the relief of the place, and to beat them in detail, this appeared the surest way to the attainment of brilliant victories. These victories actually followed, and were afterwards again repeated on a still more brilliant scale on the attempt to relieve the fortress being again renewed. We hear only one opinion on these achievements, that of unmixed admiration.

At the same time, Buonaparte could not have adopted this course on the 30th July without quite giving up the idea of the siege of Mantua, because it was impossible to save the siege train, and it could not be replaced by another in this campaign. In fact, the siege was converted into a blockade, and the town, which if the siege had continued must have very shortly fallen, held out for six months in spite of Buonaparte's victories in the open field.

Criticism has generally regarded this as an evil that was unavoidable, because critics have not been able to suggest any better course. Resistance to a relieving Army within lines of circumvallation had fallen into such disrepute and contempt that it appears to have entirely escaped consideration as a means. And yet in the reign of Louis XIV. that measure was so often used with success that we can only attribute to the force of fashion the fact that a hundred years later it never occurred to any one even to propose such a measure. If the practicability of such a plan had ever been entertained for a moment, a closer consideration of circumstances would have shown that 40,000 of the best infantry in the world under Buonaparte, behind strong lines of circumvallation round Mantua, had so little to fear from the 50,000 men coming to the relief under Wurmser, that it was very unlikely that any attempt even would be made upon their lines. We shall not seek here to establish this point, but we believe enough has been said to show that this means was one which had a right to a share of consideration. Whether Buonaparte himself ever thought of such a plan we leave undecided; neither in his memoirs nor in other sources is there any trace to be found of his having done so; in no critical works has it been touched upon, the measure being one which the mind had lost sight of. The merit of resuscitating the idea of this means is not great, for it suggests itself at once to any one who breaks loose from the trammels of fashion. Still it is necessary that it should suggest itself for us to bring it into consideration and compare it with the means which Buonaparte employed. Whatever may be the result of the comparison, it is one which should not be omitted by criticism.

When Buonaparte, in February, 1814, after gaining the battles at Etoges, Champ-Aubert, and Montmirail, left Blücher's Army, and turning upon Schwartzenberg, beat his troops at Montereau and Mormant, every one was filled with admiration, because Buonaparte, by thus throwing his concentrated force first upon one opponent, then upon another, made a brilliant use of the mistakes which his adversaries had committed in dividing their forces. If these brilliant strokes in different directions failed to save him, it was generally considered to be no fault of his, at least. No one has yet asked the question, What would have been the result if, instead of turning from Blücher upon Schwartzenberg, he had tried another blow at Blücher, and pursued him to the Rhine? We are convinced that it would have completely changed the course of the campaign, and that the Army of the Allies, instead of marching to Paris, would have retired behind the Rhine. We do not ask others to share our conviction, but no one who understands the thing will doubt, at the mere mention of this alternative course, that it is one which should not be overlooked in criticism.

In this case the means of comparison lie much more on the surface than in the foregoing, but they have been equally overlooked, because one-sided views have prevailed, and there has been no freedom of judgment.

From the necessity of pointing out a better means which might have been used in place of those which are condemned has arisen the form of criticism almost exclusively in use, which contents itself with pointing out the better means without demonstrating in what the superiority consists. The consequence is that some are not convinced, that others start up and do the same thing, and that thus discussion arises which is without any fixed basis for the argument. Military literature abounds with matter of this sort.

The demonstration we require is always necessary when the superiority of the means propounded is not so evident as to leave no room for doubt, and it consists in the examination of each of the means on its own merits, and then of its comparison with the object desired. When once the thing is traced back to a simple truth, controversy must cease, or at all events a new result is obtained, whilst by the other plan the pros and cons go on for ever consuming each other.

Should we, for example, not rest content with assertion in the case before mentioned, and wish to prove that the persistent pursuit of Blücher would have been more advantageous than the turning on Schwartzenberg, we should support the arguments on the following simple truths:

1. In general it is more advantageous to continue our blows in one and the same direction, because there is a loss of time in striking in different directions; and at a point where the moral power is already shaken by considerable losses there is the more reason to expect fresh successes, therefore in that way no part of the preponderance already gained is left idle.

2. Because Blücher, although weaker than Schwartzenberg, was, on account of his enterprising spirit, the more important adversary; in him, therefore, lay the centre of attraction which drew the others along in the same direction.

3. Because the losses which Blücher had sustained almost amounted to a defeat, which gave Buonaparte such a preponderance over him as to make his retreat to the Rhine almost certain, and at the same time no reserves of any consequence awaited him there.

4. Because there was no other result which would be so terrific in its aspects, would appear to the imagination in such gigantic proportions, an immense advantage in dealing with a Staff so weak and irresolute as that of Schwartzenberg notoriously was at this time. What had happened to the Crown Prince of Wartemberg at Montereau, and to Count Wittgenstein at Mormant, Prince Schwartzenberg must have known well enough; but all the untoward events on Blücher's distant and separate line from the Marne to the Rhine would only reach him by the avalanche of rumour. The desperate movements which Buonaparte made upon Vitry at the end of March, to see what the Allies would do if he threatened to turn them strategically, were evidently done on the principle of working on their fears; but it was done under far different circumstances, in consequence of his defeat at Laon and Arcis, and because Blücher, with 100,000 men, was then in communication with Schwartzenberg.

There are people, no doubt, who will not be convinced on these arguments, but at all events they cannot retort by saying, that "whilst Buonaparte threatened Schwartzenberg's base by advancing to the Rhine, Schwartzenberg at the same time threatened Buonaparte's communications with Paris," because we have shown by the reasons above given that Schwartzenberg would never have thought of marching on Paris.

With respect to the example quoted by us from the campaign of 1796, we should say: Buonaparte looked upon the plan he adopted as the surest means of beating the Austrians; but admitting that it was so, still the object to be attained was only an empty victory, which could have hardly any sensible influence on the fall of Mantua. The way which we should have chosen would, in our opinion, have been much more certain to prevent the relief of Mantua; but even if we place ourselves in the position of the French General and assume that it was not so, and look upon the certainty of success to have been less, the question then amounts to a choice between a more certain but less useful, and therefore less important, victory on the one hand, and a somewhat less probable but far more decisive and important victory, on the other hand. Presented in this form, boldness must have declared for the second solution, which is the reverse of what took place, when the thing was only superficially viewed. Buonaparte certainly was anything but deficient in boldness, and we may be sure that he did not see the whole case and its consequences as fully and clearly as we can at the present time.

Naturally the critic, in treating of the means, must often appeal to military history, as experience is of more value in the Art of War than all philosophical truth. But this exemplification from history is subject to certain conditions, of which we shall treat in a special chapter and unfortunately these conditions are so seldom regarded that reference to history generally only serves to increase the confusion of ideas.

We have still a most important subject to consider, which is, How far criticism in passing judgments on particular events is permitted, or in duty bound, to make use of its wider view of things, and therefore also of that which is shown by results; or when and where it should leave out of sight these things in order to place itself, as far as possible, in the exact position of the chief actor?

If criticism dispenses praise or censure, it should seek to place itself as nearly as possible at the same point of view as the person acting, that is to say, to collect all he knew and all the motives on which he acted, and, on the other hand, to leave out of the consideration all that the person acting could not or did not know, and above all, the result. But this is only an object to aim at, which can never be reached because the state of circumstances from which an event proceeded can never be placed before the eye of the critic exactly as it lay before the eye of the person acting. A number of inferior circumstances, which must have influenced the result, are completely lost to sight, and many a subjective motive has never come to light.

The latter can only be learnt from the memoirs of the chief actor, or from his intimate friends; and in such things of this kind are often treated of in a very desultory manner, or purposely misrepresented. Criticism must, therefore, always forego much which was present in the minds of those whose acts are criticised.

On the other hand, it is much more difficult to leave out of sight that which criticism knows in excess. This is only easy as regards accidental circumstances, that is, circumstances which have been mixed up, but are in no way necessarily related. But it is very difficult, and, in fact, can never be completely done with regard to things really essential.

Let us take first, the result. If it has not proceeded from accidental circumstances, it is almost impossible that the knowledge of it should not have an effect on the judgment passed on events which have preceded it, for we see these things in the light of this result, and it is to a certain extent by it that we first become acquainted with them and appreciate them. Military history, with all its events, is a source of instruction for criticism itself, and it is only natural that criticism should throw that light on things which it has itself obtained from the consideration of the whole. If therefore it might wish in some cases to leave the result out of the consideration, it would be impossible to do so completely.

But it is not only in relation to the result, that is, with what takes place at the last, that this embarrassment arises; the same occurs in relation to preceding events, therefore with the data which furnished the motives to action. Criticism has before it, in most cases, more information on this point than the principal in the transaction. Now it may seem easy to dismiss from the consideration everything of this nature, but it is not so easy as we may think. The knowledge of preceding and concurrent events is founded not only on certain information, but on a number of conjectures and suppositions; indeed, there is hardly any of the information respecting things not purely accidental which has not been preceded by suppositions or conjectures destined to take the place of certain information in case such should never be supplied. Now is it conceivable that criticism in after times, which has before it as facts all the preceding and concurrent circumstances, should not allow itself to be thereby influenced when it asks itself the question, What portion of the circumstances, which at the moment of action were unknown, would it have held to be probable? We maintain that in this case, as in the case of the results, and for the same reason, it is impossible to disregard all these things completely.

If therefore the critic wishes to bestow praise or blame upon any single act, he can only succeed to a certain degree in placing himself in the position of the person whose act he has under review. In many cases he can do so sufficiently near for any practical purpose, but in many instances it is the very reverse, and this fact should never be overlooked.

But it is neither necessary nor desirable that criticism should completely identify itself with the person acting. In War, as in all matters of skill, there is a certain natural aptitude required which is called talent. This may be great or small. In the first case it may easily be superior to that of the critic, for what critic can pretend to the skill of a Frederick or a Buonaparte? Therefore, if criticism is not to abstain altogether from offering an opinion where eminent talent is concerned, it must be allowed to make use of the advantage which its enlarged horizon affords. Criticism must not, therefore, treat the solution of a problem by a great General like a sum in arithmetic; it is only through the results and through the exact coincidences of events that it can recognise with admiration how much is due to the exercise of genius, and that it first learns the essential combination which the glance of that genius devised.

But for every, even the smallest, act of genius it is necessary that criticism should take a higher point of view, so that, having at command many objective grounds of decision, it may be as little subjective as possible, and that the critic may not take the limited scope of his own mind as a standard.

This elevated position of criticism, its praise and blame pronounced with a full knowledge of all the circumstances, has in itself nothing which hurts our feelings; it only does so if the critic pushes himself forward, and speaks in a tone as if all the wisdom which he has obtained by an exhaustive examination of the event under consideration were really his own talent. Palpable as is this deception, it is one which people may easily fall into through vanity, and one which is naturally distasteful to others. It very often happens that although the critic has no such arrogant pretensions, they are imputed to him by the reader because he has not expressly disclaimed them, and then follows immediately a charge of a want of the power of critical judgment.

If therefore a critic points out an error made by a Frederick or a Buonaparte, that does not mean that he who makes the criticism would not have committed the same error; he may even be ready to grant that had he been in the place of these great Generals he might have made much greater mistakes; he merely sees this error from the chain of events, and he thinks that it should not have escaped the sagacity of the General.

This is, therefore, an opinion formed through the connection of events, and therefore through the RESULT. But there is another quite different effect of the result itself upon the judgment, that is if it is used quite alone as an example for or against the soundness of a measure. This may be called JUDGMENT ACCORDING TO THE RESULT. Such a judgment appears at first sight inadmissible, and yet it is not.

When Buonaparte marched to Moscow in 1812, all depended upon whether the taking of the capital, and the events which preceded the capture, would force the Emperor Alexander to make peace, as he had been compelled to do after the battle of Friedland in 1807, and the Emperor Francis in 1805 and 1809 after Austerlitz and Wagram; for if Buonaparte did not obtain a peace at Moscow, there was no alternative but to return—that is, there was nothing for him but a strategic defeat. We shall leave out of the question what he did to get to Moscow, and whether in his advance he did not miss many opportunities of bringing the Emperor Alexander to peace; we shall also exclude all consideration of the disastrous circumstances which attended his retreat, and which perhaps had their origin in the general conduct of the campaign. Still the question remains the same, for however much more brilliant the course of the campaign up to Moscow might have been, still there was always an uncertainty whether the Emperor Alexander would be intimidated into making peace; and then, even if a retreat did not contain in itself the seeds of such disasters as did in fact occur, still it could never be anything else than a great strategic defeat. If the Emperor Alexander agreed to a peace which was disadvantageous to him, the campaign of 1812 would have ranked with those of Austerlitz, Friedland, and Wagram. But these campaigns also, if they had not led to peace, would in all probability have ended in similar catastrophes. Whatever, therefore, of genius, skill, and energy the Conqueror of the World applied to the task, this last question addressed to fate(*) remained always the same. Shall we then discard the campaigns of 1805, 1807, 1809, and say on account of the campaign of 1812 that they were acts of imprudence; that the results were against the nature of things, and that in 1812 strategic justice at last found vent for itself in opposition to blind chance? That would be an unwarrantable conclusion, a most arbitrary judgment, a case only half proved, because no human, eye can trace the thread of the necessary connection of events up to the determination of the conquered Princes.

(*) "Frage an der Schicksal," a familiar quotation from Schiller.—TR.

Still less can we say the campaign of 1812 merited the same success as the others, and that the reason why it turned out otherwise lies in something unnatural, for we cannot regard the firmness of Alexander as something unpredictable.

What can be more natural than to say that in the years 1805, 1807, 1809, Buonaparte judged his opponents correctly, and that in 1812 he erred in that point? On the former occasions, therefore, he was right, in the latter wrong, and in both cases we judge by the result.

All action in War, as we have already said, is directed on probable, not on certain, results. Whatever is wanting in certainty must always be left to fate, or chance, call it which you will. We may demand that what is so left should be as little as possible, but only in relation to the particular case—that is, as little as is possible in this one case, but not that the case in which the least is left to chance is always to be preferred. That would be an enormous error, as follows from all our theoretical views. There are cases in which the greatest daring is the greatest wisdom.

Now in everything which is left to chance by the chief actor, his personal merit, and therefore his responsibility as well, seems to be completely set aside; nevertheless we cannot suppress an inward feeling of satisfaction whenever expectation realises itself, and if it disappoints us our mind is dissatisfied; and more than this of right and wrong should not be meant by the judgment which we form from the mere result, or rather that we find there.

Nevertheless, it cannot be denied that the satisfaction which our mind experiences at success, the pain caused by failure, proceed from a sort of mysterious feeling; we suppose between that success ascribed to good fortune and the genius of the chief a fine connecting thread, invisible to the mind's eye, and the supposition gives pleasure. What tends to confirm this idea is that our sympathy increases, becomes more decided, if the successes and defeats of the principal actor are often repeated. Thus it becomes intelligible how good luck in War assumes a much nobler nature than good luck at play. In general, when a fortunate warrior does not otherwise lessen our interest in his behalf, we have a pleasure in accompanying him in his career.

Criticism, therefore, after having weighed all that comes within the sphere of human reason and conviction, will let the result speak for that part where the deep mysterious relations are not disclosed in any visible form, and will protect this silent sentence of a higher authority from the noise of crude opinions on the one hand, while on the other it prevents the gross abuse which might be made of this last tribunal.

This verdict of the result must therefore always bring forth that which human sagacity cannot discover; and it will be chiefly as regards the intellectual powers and operations that it will be called into requisition, partly because they can be estimated with the least certainty, partly because their close connection with the will is favourable to their exercising over it an important influence. When fear or bravery precipitates the decision, there is nothing objective intervening between them for our consideration, and consequently nothing by which sagacity and calculation might have met the probable result.

We must now be allowed to make a few observations on the instrument of criticism, that is, the language which it uses, because that is to a certain extent connected with the action in War; for the critical examination is nothing more than the deliberation which should precede action in War. We therefore think it very essential that the language used in criticism should have the same character as that which deliberation in War must have, for otherwise it would cease to be practical, and criticism could gain no admittance in actual life.

We have said in our observations on the theory of the conduct of War that it should educate the mind of the Commander for War, or that its teaching should guide his education; also that it is not intended to furnish him with positive doctrines and systems which he can use like mental appliances. But if the construction of scientific formulae is never required, or even allowable, in War to aid the decision on the case presented, if truth does not appear there in a systematic shape, if it is not found in an indirect way, but directly by the natural perception of the mind, then it must be the same also in a critical review.

It is true as we have seen that, wherever complete demonstration of the nature of things would be too tedious, criticism must support itself on those truths which theory has established on the point. But, just as in War the actor obeys these theoretical truths rather because his mind is imbued with them than because he regards them as objective inflexible laws, so criticism must also make use of them, not as an external law or an algebraic formula, of which fresh proof is not required each time they are applied, but it must always throw a light on this proof itself, leaving only to theory the more minute and circumstantial proof. Thus it avoids a mysterious, unintelligible phraseology, and makes its progress in plain language, that is, with a clear and always visible chain of ideas.

Certainly this cannot always be completely attained, but it must always be the aim in critical expositions. Such expositions must use complicated forms of science as sparingly as possible, and never resort to the construction of scientific aids as of a truth apparatus of its own, but always be guided by the natural and unbiassed impressions of the mind.

But this pious endeavour, if we may use the expression, has unfortunately seldom hitherto presided over critical examinations: the most of them have rather been emanations of a species of vanity—a wish to make a display of ideas.

The first evil which we constantly stumble upon is a lame, totally inadmissible application of certain one-sided systems as of a formal code of laws. But it is never difficult to show the one-sidedness of such systems, and this only requires to be done once to throw discredit forever on critical judgments which are based on them. We have here to deal with a definite subject, and as the number of possible systems after all can be but small, therefore also they are themselves the lesser evil.

Much greater is the evil which lies in the pompous retinue of technical terms—scientific expressions and metaphors, which these systems carry in their train, and which like a rabble-like the baggage of an Army broken away from its Chief—hang about in all directions. Any critic who has not adopted a system, either because he has not found one to please him, or because he has not yet been able to make himself master of one, will at least occasionally make use of a piece of one, as one would use a ruler, to show the blunders committed by a General. The most of them are incapable of reasoning without using as a help here and there some shreds of scientific military theory. The smallest of these fragments, consisting in mere scientific words and metaphors, are often nothing more than ornamental flourishes of critical narration. Now it is in the nature of things that all technical and scientific expressions which belong to a system lose their propriety, if they ever had any, as soon as they are distorted, and used as general axioms, or as small crystalline talismans, which have more power of demonstration than simple speech.

Thus it has come to pass that our theoretical and critical books, instead of being straightforward, intelligible dissertations, in which the author always knows at least what he says and the reader what he reads, are brimful of these technical terms, which form dark points of interference where author and reader part company. But frequently they are something worse, being nothing but hollow shells without any kernel. The author himself has no clear perception of what he means, contents himself with vague ideas, which if expressed in plain language would be unsatisfactory even to himself.

A third fault in criticism is the misuse of historical examples, and a display of great reading or learning. What the history of the Art of War is we have already said, and we shall further explain our views on examples and on military history in general in special chapters. One fact merely touched upon in a very cursory manner may be used to support the most opposite views, and three or four such facts of the most heterogeneous description, brought together out of the most distant lands and remote times and heaped up, generally distract and bewilder the judgment and understanding without demonstrating anything; for when exposed to the light they turn out to be only trumpery rubbish, made use of to show off the author's learning.

But what can be gained for practical life by such obscure, partly false, confused arbitrary conceptions? So little is gained that theory on account of them has always been a true antithesis of practice, and frequently a subject of ridicule to those whose soldierly qualities in the field are above question.

But it is impossible that this could have been the case, if theory in simple language, and by natural treatment of those things which constitute the Art of making War, had merely sought to establish just so much as admits of being established; if, avoiding all false pretensions and irrelevant display of scientific forms and historical parallels, it had kept close to the subject, and gone hand in hand with those who must conduct affairs in the field by their own natural genius.

CHAPTER VI. On Examples

Examples from history make everything clear, and furnish the best description of proof in the empirical sciences. This applies with more force to the Art of War than to any other. General Scharnhorst, whose handbook is the best ever written on actual War, pronounces historical examples to be of the first importance, and makes an admirable use of them himself. Had he survived the War in which he fell, the fourth part of his revised treatise on artillery would have given a still greater proof of the observing and enlightened spirit in which he sifted matters of experience.

But such use of historical examples is rarely made by theoretical writers; the way in which they more commonly make use of them is rather calculated to leave the mind unsatisfied, as well as to offend the understanding. We therefore think it important to bring specially into view the use and abuse of historical examples.

Unquestionably the branches of knowledge which lie at the foundation of the Art of War come under the denomination of empirical sciences; for although they are derived in a great measure from the nature of things, still we can only learn this very nature itself for the most part from experience; and besides that, the practical application is modified by so many circumstances that the effects can never be completely learnt from the mere nature of the means.

The effects of gunpowder, that great agent in our military activity, were only learnt by experience, and up to this hour experiments are continually in progress in order to investigate them more fully. That an iron ball to which powder has given a velocity of 1000 feet in a second, smashes every living thing which it touches in its course is intelligible in itself; experience is not required to tell us that; but in producing this effect how many hundred circumstances are concerned, some of which can only be learnt by experience! And the physical is not the only effect which we have to study, it is the moral which we are in search of, and that can only be ascertained by experience; and there is no other way of learning and appreciating it but by experience. In the middle ages, when firearms were first invented, their effect, owing to their rude make, was materially but trifling compared to what it now is, but their effect morally was much greater. One must have witnessed the firmness of one of those masses taught and led by Buonaparte, under the heaviest and most unintermittent cannonade, in order to understand what troops, hardened by long practice in the field of danger, can do, when by a career of victory they have reached the noble principle of demanding from themselves their utmost efforts. In pure conception no one would believe it. On the other hand, it is well known that there are troops in the service of European Powers at the present moment who would easily be dispersed by a few cannon shots.

But no empirical science, consequently also no theory of the Art of War, can always corroborate its truths by historical proof; it would also be, in some measure, difficult to support experience by single facts. If any means is once found efficacious in War, it is repeated; one nation copies another, the thing becomes the fashion, and in this manner it comes into use, supported by experience, and takes its place in theory, which contents itself with appealing to experience in general in order to show its origin, but not as a verification of its truth.

But it is quite otherwise if experience is to be used in order to overthrow some means in use, to confirm what is doubtful, or introduce something new; then particular examples from history must be quoted as proofs.

Now, if we consider closely the use of historical proofs, four points of view readily present themselves for the purpose.

First, they may be used merely as an explanation of an idea. In every abstract consideration it is very easy to be misunderstood, or not to be intelligible at all: when an author is afraid of this, an exemplification from history serves to throw the light which is wanted on his idea, and to ensure his being intelligible to his reader.

Secondly, it may serve as an application of an idea, because by means of an example there is an opportunity of showing the action of those minor circumstances which cannot all be comprehended and explained in any general expression of an idea; for in that consists, indeed, the difference between theory and experience. Both these cases belong to examples properly speaking, the two following belong to historical proofs.

Thirdly, a historical fact may be referred to particularly, in order to support what one has advanced. This is in all cases sufficient, if we have only to prove the possibility of a fact or effect.

Lastly, in the fourth place, from the circumstantial detail of a historical event, and by collecting together several of them, we may deduce some theory, which therefore has its true proof in this testimony itself.

For the first of these purposes all that is generally required is a cursory notice of the case, as it is only used partially. Historical correctness is a secondary consideration; a case invented might also serve the purpose as well, only historical ones are always to be preferred, because they bring the idea which they illustrate nearer to practical life.

The second use supposes a more circumstantial relation of events, but historical authenticity is again of secondary importance, and in respect to this point the same is to be said as in the first case.

For the third purpose the mere quotation of an undoubted fact is generally sufficient. If it is asserted that fortified positions may fulfil their object under certain conditions, it is only necessary to mention the position of Bunzelwitz(*) in support of the assertion.

(*) Frederick the Great's celebrated entrenched camp in 1761.

But if, through the narrative of a case in history, an abstract truth is to be demonstrated, then everything in the case bearing on the demonstration must be analysed in the most searching and complete manner; it must, to a certain extent, develop itself carefully before the eyes of the reader. The less effectually this is done the weaker will be the proof, and the more necessary it will be to supply the demonstrative proof which is wanting in the single case by a number of cases, because we have a right to suppose that the more minute details which we are unable to give neutralise each other in their effects in a certain number of cases.

If we want to show by example derived from experience that cavalry are better placed behind than in a line with infantry; that it is very hazardous without a decided preponderance of numbers to attempt an enveloping movement, with widely separated columns, either on a field of battle or in the theatre of war—that is, either tactically or strategically—then in the first of these cases it would not be sufficient to specify some lost battles in which the cavalry was on the flanks and some gained in which the cavalry was in rear of the infantry; and in the tatter of these cases it is not sufficient to refer to the battles of Rivoli and Wagram, to the attack of the Austrians on the theatre of war in Italy, in 1796, or of the French upon the German theatre of war in the same year. The way in which these orders of battle or plans of attack essentially contributed to disastrous issues in those particular cases must be shown by closely tracing out circumstances and occurrences. Then it will appear how far such forms or measures are to be condemned, a point which it is very necessary to show, for a total condemnation would be inconsistent with truth.

It has been already said that when a circumstantial detail of facts is impossible, the demonstrative power which is deficient may to a certain extent be supplied by the number of cases quoted; but this is a very dangerous method of getting out of the difficulty, and one which has been much abused. Instead of one well-explained example, three or four are just touched upon, and thus a show is made of strong evidence. But there are matters where a whole dozen of cases brought forward would prove nothing, if, for instance, they are facts of frequent occurrence, and therefore a dozen other cases with an opposite result might just as easily be brought forward. If any one will instance a dozen lost battles in which the side beaten attacked in separate converging columns, we can instance a dozen that have been gained in which the same order was adopted. It is evident that in this way no result is to be obtained.

Upon carefully considering these different points, it will be seen how easily examples may be misapplied.

An occurrence which, instead of being carefully analysed in all its parts, is superficially noticed, is like an object seen at a great distance, presenting the same appearance on each side, and in which the details of its parts cannot be distinguished. Such examples have, in reality, served to support the most contradictory opinions. To some Daun's campaigns are models of prudence and skill. To others, they are nothing but examples of timidity and want of resolution. Buonaparte's passage across the Noric Alps in 1797 may be made to appear the noblest resolution, but also as an act of sheer temerity. His strategic defeat in 1812 may be represented as the consequence either of an excess, or of a deficiency, of energy. All these opinions have been broached, and it is easy to see that they might very well arise, because each person takes a different view of the connection of events. At the same time these antagonistic opinions cannot be reconciled with each other, and therefore one of the two must be wrong.

Much as we are obliged to the worthy Feuquieres for the numerous examples introduced in his memoirs—partly because a number of historical incidents have thus been preserved which might otherwise have been lost, and partly because he was one of the first to bring theoretical, that is, abstract, ideas into connection with the practical in war, in so far that the cases brought forward may be regarded as intended to exemplify and confirm what is theoretically asserted—yet, in the opinion of an impartial reader, he will hardly be allowed to have attained the object he proposed to himself, that of proving theoretical principles by historical examples. For although he sometimes relates occurrences with great minuteness, still he falls short very often of showing that the deductions drawn necessarily proceed from the inner relations of these events.

Another evil which comes from the superficial notice of historical events, is that some readers are either wholly ignorant of the events, or cannot call them to remembrance sufficiently to be able to grasp the author's meaning, so that there is no alternative between either accepting blindly what is said, or remaining unconvinced.

It is extremely difficult to put together or unfold historical events before the eyes of a reader in such a way as is necessary, in order to be able to use them as proofs; for the writer very often wants the means, and can neither afford the time nor the requisite space; but we maintain that, when the object is to establish a new or doubtful opinion, one single example, thoroughly analysed, is far more instructive than ten which are superficially treated. The great mischief of these superficial representations is not that the writer puts his story forward as a proof when it has only a false title, but that he has not made himself properly acquainted with the subject, and that from this sort of slovenly, shallow treatment of history, a hundred false views and attempts at the construction of theories arise, which would never have made their appearance if the writer had looked upon it as his duty to deduce from the strict connection of events everything new which he brought to market, and sought to prove from history.

When we are convinced of these difficulties in the use of historical examples, and at the same time of the necessity (of making use of such examples), then we shall also come to the conclusion that the latest military history is naturally the best field from which to draw them, inasmuch as it alone is sufficiently authentic and detailed.

In ancient times, circumstances connected with War, as well as the method of carrying it on, were different; therefore its events are of less use to us either theoretically or practically; in addition to which, military history, like every other, naturally loses in the course of time a number of small traits and lineaments originally to be seen, loses in colour and life, like a worn-out or darkened picture; so that perhaps at last only the large masses and leading features remain, which thus acquire undue proportions.

If we look at the present state of warfare, we should say that the Wars since that of the Austrian succession are almost the only ones which, at least as far as armament, have still a considerable similarity to the present, and which, notwithstanding the many important changes which have taken place both great and small, are still capable of affording much instruction. It is quite otherwise with the War of the Spanish succession, as the use of fire-arms had not then so far advanced towards perfection, and cavalry still continued the most important arm. The farther we go back, the less useful becomes military history, as it gets so much the more meagre and barren of detail. The most useless of all is that of the old world.

But this uselessness is not altogether absolute, it relates only to those subjects which depend on a knowledge of minute details, or on those things in which the method of conducting war has changed. Although we know very little about the tactics in the battles between the Swiss and the Austrians, the Burgundians and French, still we find in them unmistakable evidence that they were the first in which the superiority of a good infantry over the best cavalry was, displayed. A general glance at the time of the Condottieri teaches us how the whole method of conducting War is dependent on the instrument used; for at no period have the forces used in War had so much the characteristics of a special instrument, and been a class so totally distinct from the rest of the national community. The memorable way in which the Romans in the second Punic War attacked the Carthaginan possessions in Spain and Africa, while Hannibal still maintained himself in Italy, is a most instructive subject to study, as the general relations of the States and Armies concerned in this indirect act of defence are sufficiently well known.

But the more things descend into particulars and deviate in character from the most general relations, the less we can look for examples and lessons of experience from very remote periods, for we have neither the means of judging properly of corresponding events, nor can we apply them to our completely different method of War.

Unfortunately, however, it has always been the fashion with historical writers to talk about ancient times. We shall not say how far vanity and charlatanism may have had a share in this, but in general we fail to discover any honest intention and earnest endeavour to instruct and convince, and we can therefore only look upon such quotations and references as embellishments to fill up gaps and hide defects.

It would be an immense service to teach the Art of War entirely by historical examples, as Feuquieres proposed to do; but it would be full work for the whole life of a man, if we reflect that he who undertakes it must first qualify himself for the task by a long personal experience in actual War.

Whoever, stirred by ambition, undertakes such a task, let him prepare himself for his pious undertaking as for a long pilgrimage; let him give up his time, spare no sacrifice, fear no temporal rank or power, and rise above all feelings of personal vanity, of false shame, in order, according to the French code, to speak the Truth, the whole Truth, and nothing but the Truth.

END OF BOOK TWO

www.ingramcontent.com/pod-product-compliance
Ingram Content Group UK Ltd.
Pitfield, Milton Keynes, MK11 3LW, UK
UKHW041828200726
13854UKWH00002BA/876

9 798710 838426